THE CHURCH FOR OTHERS

The Church for Others

Protestant Theology in
Communist East Germany

Gregory Baum

WILLIAM B. EERDMANS PUBLISHING COMPANY
GRAND RAPIDS, MICHIGAN / CAMBRIDGE, U.K.

© 1996 Wm. B. Eerdmans Publishing Co.
255 Jefferson Ave. S.E., Grand Rapids, Michigan 49503 /
P.O. Box 163, Cambridge CB3 9PU U.K.

Printed in the United States of America

01 00 99 98 97 96   7 6 5 4 3 2 1

Library of Congress Cataloging-in-Publication Data

Baum, Gregory, 1923-   .
The church for others : Protestant theology in
Communist East Germany / Gregory Baum.
          p.   cm.
Includes bibliographical references.
ISBN 0-8028-4134-1 (pbk. : alk. paper)
1. Bund der Evangelischen Kirchen in der DDR — History.
2. Protestant churches — Germany (East) — Doctrines —
History — 20th century. 3. Communism and Christianity
— Germany (East) — History — 20th century.
4. Church and state — Germany (East) — History — 20th century.
5. Germany (East) — Politics and government — 20th century.
6. Germany (East) — Church history — 20th century. I. Title.
BX4844.82.B38   1996
230'.044'0943109045 — dc20   96-43374
                                                    CIP

To Helmut Ruppel
Like-minded theologian,
ecumenist, and educator

Contents

Introduction

Thanks to a sabbatical semester granted by the Faculty of Religious Studies of McGill University, I was able to spend the entire autumn of 1992 in the now undivided Berlin, studying the Protestant theology in the former German Democratic Republic (GDR). I had heard that the Protestant Church in Communist East Germany had defined its pastoral and missionary task as "the church in socialism" (Kirche im Sozialismus), and I expected the theology that stood behind this stance to resemble Latin American liberation theology that favored a people-oriented economy and thought of itself as socialist. It turned out that I was quite wrong: the resemblance was minimal. The theology of the Protestant Church in the former GDR was a pastoral and intellectual achievement responding to a unique historical context, quite different from the Latin American situation. Because the East German Protestant theology made such a deep impression on me, I decided to write this little book to introduce the topic to a North American readership.

The changing relationship between church and state in the former GDR constituted a historical drama that made an important contribution to the eventual collapse of the Communist government. Since it is impossible to understand the meaning and power of the Protestant Church's theology without some familiarity with this extraordinary story, I devote the first chapter of this book to an account of this historical development. Because this story is so essential, I offer below — in a single long paragraph — a summary statement of this remarkable series of events. This summary will allow readers less interested in the details of this development to move directly to the subsequent chapters of the book dealing with the theology of the Protestant Church.

After a brief postwar period of pluralism in the Eastern part of Germany under Russian occupation, the creation of the GDR in 1949 produced a totally new situation. In the fifties, the Protestant Church suffered the hostility of the Communist government and underwent a certain amount of repression. In the sixties the Church became convinced that it should sever its organizational link with the West German Church; and in 1969 it created its own East German Church Federation, the Kirchenbund. The new Bund ceased lamenting the isolation of the Church in East Germany, accepted as God's will that the Church exercised its ministry in a socialist society, and began to negotiate with the government for a freer social space within which to exercise its pastoral ministry. At the end of the seventies — March 6, 1978, to be exact — an important agreement was reached between Erich Honecker, then the state president, and the representatives of the Bund, recognizing certain rights of the Protestant Church. In the eighties, this free social space of the Church, the only nonaligned organization in the entire GDR, became the home of the new citizens' movements — for peace, for environmental protection, for political dissent and alternative lifestyles — movements made up of young people who voiced their criticism of the government in less diplomatic language than did the Church. The Church shielded and defended the movements before the government; yet in order not to endanger the agreement of March 6, 1978, the Church also tried to tame the radical critics. The outspoken young people recognized that the Church protected them, yet were at the same time angry with the Church's leadership, accusing it of being overly cautious and kowtowing to the government. The movements pushed the Church to take more daring positions; and the Church, while not always pleased, continued to shield the movements. This continuing back-and-forth between Church and movements set more and more people in the local congregations into motion and eventually mobilized a majority of the population to offer nonviolent resistance to the government. This church-based mass movement brought down the Communist regime in the fall of 1989.

After chapter 1, which describes this historical development, the subsequent chapters deal with the specific topic of this book: the theology that enabled the Protestant churches in the GDR to act in unison and guided them in their important pastoral decisions. Why did the Protestant Church stop lamenting the division of Germany? Why did it come to recognize the East German Communist state? Why did it create its own federation or Kirchenbund, independent of the German Church (EKD) located in the West? Why did the Kirchenbund entertain a certain sympathy for the socialist experiment, and why did it ask Christians to cooperate with other citizens in making the GDR a more just and freedom-loving society? In the chapters following chapter 1, I wish to analyze the theological ideas and spiritual motives that prompted the Protestant Church in the obedience of faith to enter upon its bold and courageous path in the socialist society.

*   *   *

When I arrived in Berlin in September of 1992, I had no idea that the topic of my research had become the object of a heated debate in Germany. Right after the collapse of the Communist government in 1989, the Protestant Church was greatly admired in West Germany, since the mass movement that challenged the government had been organized within the local congregations. The press created the myth of a revolutionary church. But two years later, the Protestant Church found itself accused of having been a stabilizing force in the GDR, of having collaborated with an evil dictatorship, and even of having acted as spy for the government among its own people. What had happened in these two years?

The rapid reunification of Germany in 1991 was not a union of two societies where each was respected and made its own contribution to the whole. What happened was an *Anschluss,* an integration of East Germany into the existing administrative structures of West Germany. The institutions of East Germany were dismantled — *abgewickelt* (devolved) was the German euphemism — and replaced by the institutional structures of West Germany. Even the Kirchenbund was devolved: the East German Protestant Church became again members of the EKD, the church federation founded in 1945, prior to the division of Germany. An ideology emerged in the mass media, supported by politicians and intellectuals, that painted the history of the GDR in the darkest colors; denied any achievement of the socialist experiment from which Germany could learn today; discredited the creative responses made by artists, writers, and theologians in East Germany; and referred to the GDR as a dictatorship in continuity with the dictatorship of the Third Reich.

The GDR was indeed a society where public policies were dictated by the government, where economic and social institutions (apart from the church) were steered by the state bureaucracy, where civil liberties were not respected and free discussion was not allowed. But to equate the dictatorship of the GDR with that of Hitler's Germany was an attempt to disguise the horrendous crimes committed by the Nazi State, starting a war of aggression that killed millions upon millions of people and planning and executing the mass murder of six million Jews, of Gypsies and members of other nations. These crimes against humanity cannot be compared with the repression exercised by the Communist government of the GDR.

In line with this darkening of GDR history, the mass media, supported by certain intellectuals, offered a new interpretation of the church's role in the Communist society. Access to the files of Stasi, the secret police of the GDR, brought to light that the government had greatly distrusted its own citizens, suspected behind every critical remark a dangerous enemy of the state, and created a vast system of spies and informers reaching into all sectors of society, including the churches. These files revealed that pastors, priests, and lay people in the churches had acted as informal collaborators (*informelle Mitarbeiter,* IM) for the secret police. Journalists and historians, mainly from West Germany, studied these files, discovered that among the thousands of informers were prominent names — intellectuals, writers, people in high positions in various organizations, including churchmen — and broadcasted these names first in the press and subsequently in books and magazine articles. These revelations became the starting point for serious accusations against the Protestant Church, blaming the Kirchenbund of having played a stabilizing role in the Communist society, collaborated with a totalitarian government, and even acted as a watchdog for the social security police. The informers, it was claimed, did not betray the church with their action, but acted on its behalf. A perceptive article in the Swiss *Neue Zürcher Zeitung* argues that over the last two years the German mass media have replaced the old myth of the revolutionary church by a new myth of the subservient church, a fellow traveller of Communism.[1]

In response, the Protestant Church instituted its own investigation into the presence of informers among its members, and representatives of the Bund publicly defended its policy of critical solidarity.[2] While it is not my intention to review this extensive debate, I wish to make a few brief remarks. First, there were in the Protestant Church pastors, at one time organized in the so-called Pfarrerbund, who had adopted the Marxist-Leninist ideology and gave their full support to the government; but their political option and their corresponding theology were, as we shall see, consistently rejected by the Bund and the theology associated with it. Secondly, there were radicals in the citizens' movements formerly organized in the churches who were at times constrained by the Church, in some cases removed from ecclesiastical employment, and when put into prison, liberated by the Church's successful appeal to the government. Some of these dissidents, still angry with the Church, support the accusations now raised against it.

Thirdly and most importantly, the Stasi files are unreliable sources of information. The vast collection of documents gives an account of all the interviews the Stasi officers had with citizens of their choice, without revealing whether these citizens wanted to be interviewed or whether their conversation actually disclosed any secrets. To prove to their superiors how competent they were, officers tended to create the impression that their investigations were of great value to the state. Men and women in charge of institutions, including churches and seminaries, were constantly interviewed. They all had large files at the Stasi, but only a most careful reading by persons familiar with the details of the situation — not recent arrivals from West Germany — can determine whether these conversations

1. Detlev Pollak, "Die evangelischen Kirchen in der DDR," *Neue Zürcher Zeitung* (May 9/10, 1993): 27.

2. Werner Krusche, "Rückblick auf 21 Jahre Weg-Arbeitsgemeinschaft im Bund der Evangelischen Kirchen," *Sekretariat* (Berlin: Bund der Evangelischen Kirchen, 1991); Albrecht Schönherr, "Weder Opportunismus noch Opposition," *Die Zeit,* February 7, 1992, Politik, 4.

revealed any secrets, especially secrets damaging to others. The rapid judgment by the West German press on the basis of a superficial reading of the Stasi files has unjustly destroyed the reputation of several church-men, as well as several poets and artists in the GDR, among them the famous Rainer Müller and Christa Wolf.

The truth is that the Communist government looked upon the Protestant Church with great suspicion. In a book written after the collapse in 1989, Günter Schabowski, who had been a member of the government and belonged to the central committee of the Communist Party (SED), explained what his party thought of the Church, especially in the eighties:

> The surprising growth of its cultural impact made the Church an innerpolitical rival of the Party, competing with it for ideological adherence. The Church has always been a puzzle to us. Even though the number of practising Christians remained steady or even de-clined, the Church was increasingly able to become the sounding box of the universal anxiety and widely-felt discontent over the way things were going in society.[3]

It is not my task to enter into the details of this debate. What interests me in this book is the theology that guided the Protestant Church on its bold path in the socialist society. I do not disguise my admiration for the creative effort of the bishops and theologians who in fidelity to the gospel wrestled with the orientation of the Church's ministry in its new historical situation. Because of the controversy presently taking place in Germany, my book could be read as a defense of the Church's theological integrity and pastoral commitment, even though I did not intend it to be such. I simply wished to introduce the North American reader to the brilliant contextual theology that steered a Protestant Church through an important period of its history.

*   *   *

Catholics in East Germany were a small minority. They constituted what Germans call a church of the diaspora. The narrow Eichsfeld in

---

3. Günter Schabowski, *Der Absturz* (Berlin: Rowohl, 1991), 162.

Thuringia was the only traditionally Catholic region in the GDR. Some Catholics lived in the industrialized parts where their families had moved one or two generations ago. But the majority of Catholics had settled in the GDR after World War II, arriving from German territories beyond the border, especially from Silesia. In 1964, 87% of the East German population was Protestant and 11% Catholic.[4]

The Catholic Church in the GDR did not follow the path of the Protestant Church, but preferred to remain aloof from the socialist society and concentrate its pastoral efforts on protecting and invigorating the parishes spread across the country. There were several reasons for this. Because it was a small, diaspora community, not a Volkskirche, the Catholic Church did not feel responsible for the whole of society. Because Catholics on the whole did not have their roots in the GDR, they retained a stronger cultural bond with West German Catholics. Because the Catholic Church was a part of a world church, its policies were not simply determined by the requirements of its historical situation. The Catholics in the GDR did not produce their own contextual theology, in part because the bishops followed a cautious approach, and in part because as a small minority they did not have the rich intellectual resources enjoyed by the Protestants.

Yet it would be quite wrong to generalize and suppose that all Catholics in the GDR had been withdrawn and cautious. Just as Protestants had the Pfarrerbund that supported the Communist regime, so Catholics had their government supporters, a group that published the monthly, *Begegnung,* and organized a yearly international conference at Berlin, die Kirchenkonferenz katholischer Christen. More significant and more interesting is that from the late sixties on, Catholic student organizations and several parishes, influenced by Vatican Council II, politely expressed their disagreement with the bishops' cautious policy and sought a new, critical-constructive approach to their society, similar to the Protestant path. In this endeavor they were supported by some priests and occasionally by a bishop. The experience of these Catholics is a story that deserves to be told. Yet since the focus of this book is not history, but theology — the contextual theology of the GDR — I

4. Robert F. Goeckel, *The Lutheran Church and the East-German State* (Ithaca, NY: Cornell University Press, 1990), 9.

shall not deal with the Catholic presence in that country. Let me add, however, that I greatly appreciated meeting some of these critical Catholics in East Germany and gratefully received the spontaneous friendship they extended to me.

*   *   *

Before turning to the history of the evolving church-state relations in the GDR, I must explain to North American readers why the Protestant Church and the Catholic Church in the GDR were obliged to engage in constant negotiations with the government. There were three reasons for this.

First, in a state that does not recognize civil liberties, in particular the freedoms of peaceful assembly and independent organization — and the GDR was such a state — a church is in need of government permission for all of its pastoral activities. While freedom of conscience and freedom of worship were guaranteed by the constitution of the GDR, special permission was required for pastoral activities other than worship, such as holding educational meetings; supporting academies and seminaries; printing parish bulletins, church papers, and ecclesiastical reviews; importing theological texts from outside the country; repairing or building churches; planning nation-wide conferences and participating at international congresses; receiving alms in foreign currency, especially the substantial sums from the West German Church; and so forth. The Protestant Church was constantly engaged in bargaining with the government in order to pursue its pastoral ministry. The same was true of the Catholic Church. Even though the Catholic Church represented a minority in the country and tried to remain as aloof as possible, in the absence of civil liberties the hierarchy was obliged to carry on endless negotiations with the government.

Second, the Protestant Church and the Catholic Church in the old Germany had been fully integrated into society and exercised within it important social functions, to a large extent with the help of public funds. This remained true even in the GDR. Thus, despite the repression of the fifties, in 1960 the Protestant Church in the GDR still operated 51 hospitals, 89 homes for the retarded, 226 nursing homes, 11 homes for infants, 21 orphanages, 117 retreat centers, 12 hotels,

326 kindergartens, and 19 special daycare centers for the'retarded.[5] The Church was then employing 50,000 people. Since the funds for these institutions came to a large extent from the state, representing a substantial part of the GDR's health care budget, regular negotiations with several government ministries were inevitable.

A third characteristic of the Protestant Church in East Germany was that it had been the church of the great majority and regarded itself as the "Volkskirche" — that is, as representing the nation and speaking on its behalf. Even though secularization was taking place at a rapid pace, the Protestant Church continued to think of itself as responsible for the nation's well-being and hence addressed the government on the human issues of concern to the entire population. This reminded me of the attitude of the Catholic Church in Quebec, where I now live, which also had been a *Volkskirche,* a church representing a nation, and which, despite the ongoing secularization and the drastic decline of membership, continues to feel responsible for the nation and addresses society and the government on issues of human well-being.[6]

The translations from the German in this book are my own unless otherwise indicated. Occasionally I offer a free, rather than a literal translation, to bring out more clearly the thrust and meaning of the original.

5. Goeckel, 21-22.
6. See Gregory Baum, *The Church in Quebec* (Montreal: Novalis, 1991).

CHAPTER 1

Church-State Relations in the GDR[1]

After the end of the Second World War in 1945, Germany came under the control of the Allies. In 1949, two separate German republics were created, West Germany, named the German Federal Republic (GFR) under the auspices of the Western Allies; and East Germany, named the German Democratic Republic (GDR) under the auspices of the Soviets. Between 1945 and 1949, the eastern part of Germany, then directly under Soviet control, enjoyed democratic freedoms and political pluralism. The Soviets honored all forces in Germany that had resisted fascism: the political parties — Communist, Socialist, and Christian Democratic (the latter being the heir of the pre-war Centre Party) — as well as the churches represented by antifascist personalities who had suffered under Hitler. For four years the East Germans enjoyed a climate of dialogue and cooperation. The National Committee for a Free Germany and the Free German Youth Organization had Christian members, some of them prominent church leaders. The Soviets allowed the churches to undertake their own denazification procedures. When, in 1946, the Communist and Socialist parties united to form the Socialist Unity Party, in German abbreviated as SED, Protestant ministers,

---

1. In this chapter I follow closely, but not exclusively, Robert Goeckel's excellent study, *The Lutheran Church and the East German State: Political Conflict and Change under Ulbricht and Honecker* (Ithaca, NY: Cornell University Press, 1990). References to this book will be given parenthetically in the text.

1

formerly members of the Socialist Party, remained in the new formation. At that time, the SED still stood for democratic pluralism.

*   *   *

The situation began to change soon after the creation of the German Democratic Republic (GDR). The constitution of the new state still echoed the model of the Weimar Republic dismantled by Hitler in 1933. The constitution guaranteed the freedom of faith and the autonomy of the churches, and it recognized the churches as public institutions with certain privileges, such as the teaching of religion in the schools, the raising of the church tax, access to hospitals and prisons, and the right to certain subsidies.

However the ruling party, the SED, gradually became Stalinized: it came to look upon itself as a party in a new sense, as the authoritative political institution, admitting no rivals, responsible for the socialist transformation of society as a whole. The SED became a Communist party, obedient to Soviet guidance. The efforts of certain members to resist the Soviet model and defend a German path to socialism was condemned as "Titoism" and led to severe purges. Stalinization also meant the nationalization of all industries and the central planning of the economy.

Yet the SED decided not to abolish the other political parties, but rather to bring them under its control and use them as agents to promote the official doctrine in sectors of the population not identified with the industrial working class. These were called "the bloc parties." The Christian Democratic Party (abbreviated in German as CDU) was to urge the official message upon church people; the Peasant Party, upon the farm population; and the Liberal Democratic Party, upon the secular middle classes. We shall see further on that despite the effort of the CDU to influence the churches, and despite the willing collaboration of certain Protestant ministers and Catholic spokesmen, the churches consistently refused to support or ally itself with the Christian Democratic bloc party.

In the fifties, the Communist state began a hostile campaign against the churches. It introduced compulsory atheist teaching in the schools and created a youth dedication rite (Jugendweihe), a secular replacement of confirmation, which it urged young people to receive. The government also addressed the entire population to communicate atheist socialist ideas and promote atheist socialist values. Because in exercising their pastoral ministry the churches depended on govern- ment-granted permissions — we saw what this meant in the introduc- tion — the government was able to control the churches by curtailing their activities. The government used a system of rewards and punish- ments that greatly limited the freedom of the church. In addition to that, the government kept secret files on young Christians who dis- sented from the official ideology and prevented them from entering university or even the higher grades of secondary school. This was against the law, which guaranteed equality independently of religion or ethnic origin, yet it was commonly practiced. If people had private access to highly placed party members and put in a complaint, they often saw the situation rectified; but there existed no court to which people could appeal.

At the same time, the East German government did not follow the Soviet model of church persecution. No churches or seminaries were ever closed, and no church leaders were put into prison. The church's internal autonomy was weakened, but not wholly taken away. Sunday worship and parish life continued without interruption. The churches held their meetings, decided upon policy, and made their own decisions. Because the church was able to survive even during the most difficult years of the fifties, it did not advocate political opposition to the government. Most Christians may not have agreed with the decla- ration of Otto Dibelius, the outspoken bishop of Berlin, that the GDR was not a legally constituted state and that consequently people did not have to obey its laws, not even the traffic regulations (Goeckel, 620). Still, in the fifties most Christians tended to believe that the Communist regime would have a short life and that the return of a united, democratic Germany was not far away.

The question poses itself: Why among all the Warsaw Pact coun- tries did East Germany adopt by far the most "liberal" approach to the Christian church? There are three reasons for this. First, there was the so-called concentration camp effect, the memory of suffering shared by Communists and Christians in Hitler's concentration camps. Already in the thirties, assemblies of exiled German Communists had made public declarations acknowledging the church's opposition to fascism. Second, the government thought that since the church was Protestant in East Germany — the only Communist country with a Protestant majority — it would be more flexible and adaptable than the more traditional Orthodox and Catholic churches. Third, the government shied away from persecuting the church because it eagerly sought the recognition of the GDR by the West German state and hence wanted to make a good impression.

In the early fifties, most Christians were still attached to German unity. They looked upon the Protestant Church of Germany (EKD) as the symbol of national unity and as a bridge between East and West. Yet as the years went by, a growing number of Christians began to look upon the GDR as their home and their country. They acquired with their socialist fellow citizens a new East German national identity. Some Christians even turned to the official socialism. In 1958 a group of Protestant ministers founded the clergy association, the Pfarrer-bund, which endorsed the Marxist-Leninist philosophy of the SED. Others, not committed to this orthodoxy, became members of the Christian Peace Conference founded in Prague in 1958 by Josef Hromádka. But even Christians who did not have the same sympathy for socialism no longer wanted to define themselves as the poor brothers of the wealthy West Germans, but preferred to be proud citizens of their own country.

After the GDR was recognized by the Soviet Union in 1954, the government was eager to be recognized as an autonomous state by the international community. To do this, it had to demonstrate that it had no institutional link with West Germany; in other words, that there existed two distinct German states. The policy of stressing the separation from West Germany was called *Abgrenzung*, in English, 'delimitation.' In the name of this *Abgrenzung*, the government urged the regional Protestant churches to separate themselves from the inter-German Protestant Church (EKD). When, in 1958, the EKD made an agreement on military chaplains with the West German government, the East German government increased its polemics against the EKD as "the NATO Church" and refused to enter into negotiations with representatives of that church. The East German church leaders decided to address the GDR government in their "Kommuniqué," published in

1958, in which they support the GDR's peace initiatives and "the development toward socialism." Since the East German bishops were not in total agreement about what this meant, and since some of them, nobably Mitzenheim and Krummacher, publicly expressed their "respect for socialism," the government preferred to negotiate directly with individual bishops. Because of these pressures, the regional churches in the GDR began to plan the creation of their own independent church federation that would enable them to find a united voice, resist the attempts of the government to deal separately with each regional church, and express both their spiritual solidarity with the EKD and their institutional independence from it. This process began in 1958 and ended with the creation in 1969 of a federation, the *Kirchenbund* or *Bund.*

Political pressure was, as we shall see further on, not the only reason for setting up the Bund. A growing number of churchmen believed that a church was bound to exercise its ministry in the society in which God's providence has placed it. The Protestant Church in the GDR should therefore discourage Christians from being sentimentally attached to the past and practicing an interior emigration from society: the Church should in faith recognize its place, define its mission, serve the people and their society, and encourage Christians to assume responsibility for their world.

*   *   *

In the sixties, the new pastoral attitude received growing support in the Protestant Church. At the same time, the government itself became less hostile to the church. When the West German government adopted a more open approach to the Soviet bloc countries, the government of the GDR was afraid that it would be left in the lurch by these countries as they sought financial support from West Germany. This fear of isolation prompted the government to intensify its policy of *Abgrenzung.* As more and more East Germans traveled westward, the government decided to build the Berlin Wall in 1961. Already before that event, in October 1960, Walter Ulbricht, the state president, publicly acknowledged that "Christianity and the humanistic goals of socialism are not contradictory," seemingly pleading for the loyalty of Christians to the socialist society. In February 1961, Ulbricht entertained a long conversation with Emil Fuchs, a professor of theology at the University of Leipzig, who supported socialist economics. At this occasion Fuchs handed Ulbricht a declaration signed by 20,000 church workers, clergy and laity, that recognized the common, humanistic responsibility of Christians and Marxists, urged greater cooperation, supported the government's peace initiatives, and criticized West German government policy (Goeckel, 60). A second conversation took place in April 1964, this time between Ulbricht and Bishop Mitzenheim of Thuringia, in which the latter expressed respect for the state and called for greater cooperation.

At the same time, the Protestant Church's new pastoral approach was receiving growing support from the local congregations. In 1963 the Lutheran Churches (VELK) and the Churches of the Union (EKU) published "Ten Articles on the Church's Freedom and Service," later endorsed by the church leadership conference, which contained the following text:

> In existing social conditions we must ascertain what God wants from us and do good according to his will. We fall prey to a lack of faith if we assume that God has abandoned us in the existing conditions and thus begin to doubt, or if we interpret the historical and social circumstances as the direct gift of the will of God and accept them without reservation. (Goeckel, 63)

The church leaders discussed what "respect for socialism" meant and pleaded with Christians "to avoid the alternatives of resignation and accommodation."

The Weissensee Study Circle, a respected clergy association in Berlin, exercised spiritual and theological leadership in the church. The members reflected on the present situation of the church in the context of its history: they were critical of the church's past, its identification with the Prussian monarchy, its lack of support for the Weimar Republic, and its compromised behavior under the Hitler regime. Their repentance detached them from the church's past and moved them to adopt a positive attitude to their present society, at least to the extent that it stood for equality and social justice. Their "Seven Theological Theses," published in 1963, contained this text:

Faith in the love of God makes us free to cooperate in the social order and to take on responsibility. Christians and non-Christians work together at the task of creating internally a humane and just order and a lasting peace in the relations among peoples and states. (Goeckel, 63)

At the same time, the churches in East Germany wanted to retain their membership in the larger German Church, the EKD, even though the Communist government pressured them to make themselves independent. Walter Ulbricht had this to say: "The Church in the GDR spreads the principles of humanism in Christian responsibility. Many Christians in West Germany share the same goals, but their bishops have made the Church a military Church and support the policy of the German Federal Republic." The same message was delivered by Gerald Götting, the leader of the East German CDU — one of the bloc parties mentioned above. When the Synod of the EKD met in Fürstenwalde (East Germany) in 1967, the decision was made, despite that pressure, to remain united. Yet the final resolution stated that the member churches of the EKD were obliged to serve in the part of Germany in which they lived, West or East, and that they always had to respect the interests of the other side in their decisions. Fürstenwalde upheld the unity of the EKD, but in fact provided pastoral arguments for a separation.

At this time the SED government was preparing a new constitution, one that was to reflect more truly the Communist orientation of the state. (The first constitution of 1949 still echoed the spirit of the liberal-democratic Weimar Republic.) The proposal for the new constitution was more restrictive regarding the churches. Religion was only mentioned in an article affirming equal rights and forbidding discrimination for reasons of ethnicity, race, or religion. The churches were no longer recognized as public institutions. They no longer had complete internal autonomy, but had to order their activities in agreement with the constitution and the legal requirements of the GDR.

In this situation, a common voice of the churches in the GDR became an urgent necessity. In February, 1968, the Protestant bishops met at Kloster Lehnin, an old monastery building close to Berlin, to discuss the proposal for the new constitution and to formulate a common response addressed to the government. In the so-called Letter from Lehnin, the bishops delivered a strong statement demanding freedom for the church, but were silent on the topic of inter-German unity and the EKD. Some bishops went further in expressing their loyalty to the GDR. Bishops Krusche and Mitzenheim acknowledged that the borders of a country should also define the borders of the churches. Bishop Krummacher called for the international recognition of the GDR and the universal acceptance of the postwar borders. Other bishops were more cautious.

Despite previous threats, Walter Ulbricht listened to the Letter from Lehnin and introduced small modifications in the constitutional proposal. He added a paragraph that protected religious confessions from discrimination. He also added the sentence, "Further agreements between church and state could be subject to separate negotiations." Ulbricht recognized two activities to which the churches were entitled: the spiritual ministry to their members and actions useful for the community as a whole. These were minimal concessions. The churches regretted the absence of any definitiveness: the new law was neither a clear separation of church and state, nor a concordat granting the church legal rights. Promised were only ongoing negotiations. Still, when the referendum on the constitution was held later in 1968, the Protestant pastors did not boycott it or ask their people to do so. In fact, the new constitution was massively supported by the East German population.

What worried the church leaders was that the government might negotiate with the regional churches to undermine their unity. They set up a commission on church structure, chaired by Albrecht Schönherr, which was to plan the creation of an East German church federation capable of speaking in a single voice for all the regional churches (Goeckel, 76-78). Although this commission was still under the EKD, it was given the authority to make a proposal to the East German churches. Schönherr offered a theological argument to convince the East German churchmen who still preferred to remain in the EKD: he proposed that church structures are meant to serve the witness of the church, and that if they can no longer do this, they would have to be changed. The church's witness has priority over its structure. The commission recommended that the new Bund retain a strong bond with the EKD, even if this bond was spiritual and doctrinal rather than organizational. This was a controversial article. Many churchmen felt that it betrayed the demands of unity for political reasons, while others — and more especially the government — were displeased with the affirmation of a close bond with the EKD. Schönherr's great skill in finding mediating formulas and creating consensus among the churches eventually convinced the church leaders to set up the new, independent Kirchenbund. The EKD was not pleased; however, it accepted the separation as regrettable, but necessary. The Kirchenbund, set up in 1969, defined itself as "a community of witness and service" in the GDR. Its founding document included article 4,4 expressing its continuing bond with the West German Church.[2]

*   *   *

The government did not recognize the Kirchenbund until two years later. One objection was the continuing link to the EKD which, according to the government's interpretation, showed that the Protestant Church still regarded itself as the bridge between the two Germanies. In response, Schönherr persuaded the government that this link was understood in spiritual, not material terms. Another objection, reflecting the same concern with *Abgrenzung,* was the geographical contours of the Church of Berlin-Brandenburg, which included West Berlin, part of the GFR. Following an intense debate, the Church eventually decided to recognize two bishops of Berlin: Kurt Scharf, the former bishop remaining in West Berlin, and Albrecht Schönherr, the new bishop of Berlin-Brandenburg in the GDR. After the clarification of several other issues, the government recognized the Kirchenbund in 1971.

This recognition was a mixed blessing. For now the government expected the Protestant Church to follow a new orientation, which meant — among other things — to express its loyalty to the country and support the international recognition of the GDR. The government also asked for greater cooperation of Christians in the building a socialist

2. Reinhard Henkys, *Bund der evangelischen Kirchen in der DDR. Dokumente zu seiner Entstehung* (Berlin: Eckart Verlag, 1970), 35.

society. While the government kept stressing the unbridgeable ideological distance between its materialist philosophy and the Christian world-
view, it nonetheless wanted the Church to stand for the socialism of
the SED.

Since the Bund understood itself as "a community of witness and
service" in its society, it wanted to be loyal to the GDR and not define
itself as the opposition to the government. Acting as president of the
Bund, Schönherr made several gestures of cooperation. He supported
the membership of the GDR in the United Nations Organization as
well as the government's proposal for stabilizing peace in Europe. The
government was also pleased that through the World Council of
Churches (WCC), the Bund supported liberation movements in the
Third World. The Bund also explained that the Church did not ask
for the restoration of its traditional privileges: all it wanted was to serve
God in a free and unhindered way through public witness and service
to the community. The Bund rejected withdrawal from society and
stood for increasing cooperation.

At the same time, the Kirchenbund continued to remind the
government that the equality guaranteed by the Constitution was not
respected in actual practice. Christians continued to suffer discrimination, young people were excluded from higher education, local congregations were hindered in the free exercise of their ministry, and churches
were prevented by government censorship from importing religious and
theological literature of their choice. In many places all over the country,
Christians were treated as second-class citizens.

The Bund also refused the request to support socialism. The
Synod held at Eisenach in 1971 proposed a formula that the Bund
adopted and defended throughout its history. According to the Synod,
the Church was "*nicht neben, nicht gegen, sondern im Sozialismus*" —
"not beside, not against, but in socialism." The Synod thus rejected
two possibilities: that the Church withdraw into a separate ghetto
existence, and that it define itself as opposition in the socialist society.
The Synod affirmed the ministry of the Church "in" but not "for"
socialism. The government was not satisfied with this: it wanted the
Church to declare its adherence to socialist ideology and practice.

What precisely did "*Kirche im Sozialismus*" mean? We shall see
further on that Christians interpreted this statement with the help of

several theological themes: while a few spoke of the Christian duty to obey the government, the greater number preferred to speak of the church's vocation in society. They interpreted the church's mission as the call to announce God's claim on the whole of society, or to serve the realization of God's shalom, or to become the Church-for-others, or to practice critical solidarity, or to walk the narrow path between refusal and accommodation. When, at the Synod of 1972 held at Dresden, Heino Falcke spoke of the hope Christians entertained for an "improvable socialism," the government regarded this as heresy and demanded that the Church not record his speech in the synodal proceedings.

The back-and-forth between the Protestant Church and the government continued. The Church gained greater freedom: it compromised on certain issues, while on others it strengthened its critical stance. The following is an example of compromise. Although in the fifties churches threatened to exclude from confirmation young people who had received the youth dedication rite (Jugendweihe), from the sixties on, churches became more tolerant. Because young Christians regarded the rite as a harmless secular ceremony necessary for their advancement in society, the Church reluctantly agreed to confirm them (Goeckel, 236-237).

Yet there were also examples of increasing criticism. After the Church's pleading that the pacifist conscience of young people be respected, the government in 1964 introduced a new category in the military, the so-called *Bausoldaten,* soldiers who served as builders, not as arms-bearers. Yet from the seventies on, the Church asked the government for more: it pleaded — in vain this time — for a pacifist alternative to military service. When the government in 1975 supported the anti-Israel resolution of the United Nations calling Zionism racism, the Church, recalling the awful history of Nazi antisemitism, introduced in its congregations the commemoration of November 9, 1938, the night of the broken glass, the burning of the synagogues (Goeckel, 208).

Erich Honecker, state president since 1971, while strongly committed to Marxism-Leninism, came to believe that the Protestant Church could become useful to the state in several ways. Since the government in the seventies wanted to combine *Abgrenzung* against West Germany with a good-neighbor policy, Honecker believed the Church, with its West German connection, might be of help. At the same time, growing unrest was spreading within the GDR. After the Helsinki resolutions on human rights were signed by the nations of the Warsaw Pact in 1975, a hundred thousand East Germans, invoking the newly proclaimed right to emigrate, demanded permission to leave the country. At the same time, the artistic and intellectual communities, largely socialist in orientation, were becoming increasingly critical of the government. Rolf Biermann was sent into exile in 1977. The government wondered whether in this situation the Protestant Church might become a stabilizing factor. But the Church did not allow itself to be bought. Schönherr insisted that the relationship of church and state must be judged by what happens at the base in each locality, and there discrimination and exclusion still occurred. The Church, Schönherr said, could never become an obedient messenger boy for the state (as were the bloc parties), even if the Church was not — as some Communists feared — the Trojan horse of the counterrevolution steered by Western powers.

On March 6, 1978, Erich Honecker and his advisers met the executive officers of the Kirchenbund to reach an agreement between government and Church. The state was willing to grant a series of concessions in the hope that the Church would stand for loyalty to the GDR and help to legitimate the GDR on the international level. The Church received permission to broadcast television programs six times a year; it obtained access to prisons, was allowed to build churches in new industrial settlements, was guaranteed state pensions for church workers, was promised state cooperation in organizing its congresses (trains, buses, halls, etc.), was granted greater freedom to publish ecclesiastical material, and got permission to invite the Central Committee of the WCC to hold its meeting of 1981 in Dresden.

However, the agreement was not a legal act: no binding document was published that would allow the Church to insist on its rights. Still, the concessions made by the state did create a certain free space for the Church with access to means of communication and transportation, in which — as it turned out — it was possible for critical groups to organize and start a mass movement.

Some pastors were unhappy with the agreement of March 6, believing that the Church had compromised itself,[3] but the bishops

---

3. A high-strung pastor named Brüsewitz decided to demonstrate his opposition by burning himself.

who were usually more critical of the existing order than Schönherr, such as Bishops Fränkel, Hempel, and Krusche, approved of the agreement; and thanks to their support, it was endorsed by the Synod of 1978. Despite different tendencies in the churches, Albrecht Schönherr always succeeded in achieving consensus, preserving unity and allowing the Bund to address the local congregations and the wider public in a single voice.

*   *   *

In the eighties a new phase of church-state relations began. While the first generation of Communists in the GDR looked back to rich experiences, to the German socialist movement beginning in the late nineteenth century and later to the ardent struggle against Hitler's fascism, the subsequent generation no longer had these memories. The Communist state now searched more deeply for cultural roots in German history and even turned to the Christian past. The government decided to rebuild some of the great churches which had been destroyed in the War and reinstate Luther as a man of destiny and a German hero. The government even invited the Church to cooperate in the public celebration of the 500th anniversary of Luther's birth in 1983. The Kirchenbund, true to its style, decided after some hesitation to join the government, and at the same time to prepare its own independent commemoration, ecumenical in spirit and international in outreach. A few years later, in 1987, the state celebrated the 750th anniversary of Berlin with the restoration of the old St. Nicholas quarter, including the St. Nicholas Church, and the completion of the repairs at the Protestant Cathedral, the Berliner Dom.

Yet disquieting for the government in those years was the emergence of new social movements, young people organized in the local churches, that supported the protection of the environment, opposed nuclear weapons and the militaristic spirit, defended human rights, and demanded greater personal freedom.

Stirred by its participation in the World Council of Churches, the East German Church expressed its concern over the deteriorating environment already in the seventies, even though the topic was taboo in the GDR at that time. In the eighties the Church created an environmental research center at Wittenberg. In the same period, eco-logical base groups were formed in the local congregations, involving many people who previously had little contact with the Church. These groups involved themselves in educating the public, disseminating in-formation, organizing public protests, and articulating direct criticism of the government in a manner hitherto unacceptable in the GDR. After the accident at Chernobyl in 1986, they vigorously opposed the nuclear program of the government. The 1987 Peace Workshop in Berlin was held under the motto, "Chernobyl is everywhere."

The government was unwilling to accept this form of direct criticism. Even the Church, loyal to the agreement of March 6, 1978, was embarrassed by the aggressive words and gestures of the grassroots, so different from its own constant, but subtle and diplomatic critique of the government. Sometimes the Church tried to tame the protesters. When Jochen Rochau, a church worker in Halle, organized a bicycle parade through the polluted industrial areas near the city, with riders wearing gas masks and holding protest signs, the government inter-vened, and the Church decided to terminate Rochau's employment (Goeckel, 255).

A similar development took place in relation to the peace move-ment. Supported by the ecumenical connection with the WCC, the East German Church promoted peace and opposed nuclear weapons already in the sixties. But when, at the end of the seventies, the arms race escalated, NATO decided to install middle-range nuclear missiles, and the GDR gradually became a more militarized society, the Church renewed its peace efforts. It protested — unsuccessfully — against the introduction of military instruction as a compulsory subject in the secondary schools of the GDR. The position of the Church was not radical: it did not advocate unconditional, unilateral disarmament, but more moderately urged (as did many American churches) a process of negotiated mutual disarmament. Still, the Communist government decided to curtail the Church's involvement in peace education. After the massive protest movement in Poland, the government of the GDR tried to stop the Church's independent peace movement altogether. During Peace Week in November 1980, the Church was forbidden to ring the bells.

The effect of these measures was the opposite of what the govern-ment intended. More and more young people joined the peace movement, organized groups in the local congregations, and protested against government policy. In May 1981, the movement submitted a petition with thousands of signatures asking the government for a peaceful alternative to military service — a social peace service to the community, longer than the required military service. Yet the answer was No. Military training, the government explained, served defense, not war. Since the government feared nuclear war and stood for coexistence and peace, the Church felt that it would be unjust to accuse it of promoting war and to label young people who joined the army as sinners. According to a formulation of several church leaders, including Schönherr, both training in the army and seeking an exemption served the cause of peace — but seeking an exemption gave "the clearer signal" (Goeckel, 262). The government was outraged. It made a new effort to stop the peace movement under the Church's auspices. An occasion arrived when the planners of Peace Week 1981 prepared badges saying "Swords into Ploughshares" that were to be worn by all participants. Even though this biblical image had been used in a Soviet sculpture given to the United Nations, the government decided that wearing this sign was an action hostile to the state. The police intervened during Peace Week and pulled off the badges by force. The Church then protested against the curtailment of its freedom.

The dynamic interaction continued between the Church and the peace movement organized within it. Sometimes the Church supported it. When in 1982 a silent march of peace activists in Dresden was violently interrupted by the police, the minister of the Kreuzkirche invited the marchers to seek refuge in the spacious church and discuss the future of the peace movement. At other times the Church tried to tame the movement. The Berlin Appeal, a public action organized by a Protestant pastor, Rainer Eppelmann, and supported by two thousand men and women, demanded immediate disarmament, the withdrawal of foreign troops from German lands both East and West, and the right of Germans to decide upon their future. Since the Appeal challenged the very foundation of the GDR, the Church of Berlin-Brandenburg dissociated itself from it, even though it recognized that it expressed people's longing for peace. Still, the Church intervened to protect Eppelmann, and to have him released from prison and freed from further prosecution (Goeckel, 363).

In the subsequent years, the restlessness of the population increased. Tens of thousands of East Germans decided to leave the country. The Church tried to persuade people to stay at home. What do you seek in the West? the Church asked. Is it consumer goods and material satisfaction? If you love freedom as Christians understand it, you should not leave, but stay to work for a socialist society in which Christians can be truly at home.

In 1985 the Gorbachev phenomenon in the Soviet Union exercised an enormous influence upon the population of the GDR. The government strongly resisted the call for *peristroika,* and while it continued the rhetoric of loyalty to Soviet leadership, it actually tightened its control over culture and further limited the range of public debate. Gorbachev's speeches had to be smuggled in from West Germany.

One consequence of the new restlessness was that more and more people joined the citizens' movements organized in the local congregations, the only places in the GDR where open discussion could be carried on. The leadership of the Church was now being challenged by "the church from below" that was becoming increasingly impatient. The citizens' movements now dealt not only with the issues of ecology and peace, but with a wider agenda of democratic rights and alternative lifestyles. The Kirchenbund created a study commission, Our Congregations and Their Groups, chaired by Heino Falcke, that eventually recommended that the Church remain open to those who wish to organize within it, even if it cannot approve of all their views (Goeckel, 268-269). The Church should continue to shield the group members, even when it does not support certain of their positions.

But the tension continued. The movements became increasingly active, produced newsletters and other literature, and exercised a wide influence on the public. Some of their members accused the church leadership of compliance and cowardice. The Church itself became somewhat divided: some congregations remained open to the groups; while others felt that the group's political involvement disturbed their community of worship. Since in response to the growing unrest the government increased its effort to control the public, if need be by force, the church leadership, especially in Berlin, withdrew from some of the protest activities. In 1987 the Church of Berlin-Brandenburg cancelled the carefully planned Peace Week to prevent police violence.

Yet later in the same year, the security forces invaded a Berlin congregation, arrested the activists, confiscated their printing press, and accused them of plotting against the state. The increasing violence used by the government in turn angered the leaders of the Church and strengthened their support for the movements.

A worldwide ecumenical undertaking — the so-called Conciliar Process — proposed by the East German Church at the Vancouver Assembly of the WCC in 1983, became a powerful mobilizing force in the GDR. From 1986 on, the East German Church involved its people in the preparation for a European ecumenical assembly in Basel on "Justice, Peace and the Integrity of Creation" in May 1989 and for the worldwide assembly of the WCC in Seoul on the same topic in March 1990. To prepare for these international events, the Church in the GDR planned three large assemblies, in February and October 1988 and in April 1989. Delegates from all parts of the country brought briefs and reports from their groups or their congregations. The Catholic bishops eventually gave permission for Catholics to participate in this process. The immediate aim was to compose a final document that would critically examine the GDR in the light of the demands of justice, peace, and the care for the natural environment. This unheard-of undertaking generated nationwide interest and created greater unity between the churches and the citizens' movements.

In September of 1989, people gathered by the thousands in the city congregations all over the GDR to stage nonviolent demonstrations protesting against the inflexibility of the government. What took place was a peaceful revolution by the masses, by people who carried candles and stood in silence, who risked their lives facing police and army, and refused to move until the country was paralyzed and the government was willing to give in and negotiate. This was the end of the dictatorship.

CHAPTER 2

The Theology of the Kirchenbund

The subject of this study is the theology that allowed the Protestant Church in the GDR to speak in a single voice and that acted as a guide in the making of its bold pastoral decisions. Why did the Protestant Church stop lamenting the division of Germany? Why did it decide to recognize the East German Communist state? Why did it create its own Kirchenbund independent of the German Church (EKD) located in the West? Why did the Kirchenbund entertain a certain sympathy for the socialist experiment, and why did it ask Christians to cooperate with other citizens in making East Germany a more just and more freedom-loving socialist society?

It is not at all obvious that such a theology in the singular existed in the Protestant Church of East Germany. The Bund was, after all, a federation of regional churches with different doctrinal and cultural backgrounds; and a plurality of theological opinions existed even within each member church. The Bund was actually proud of its theological pluralism. In an address of 1973, Bishop Werner Krusche proposed that pluralism in the church has a theological foundation. Pluralism is grounded in the love of God, who addresses and reaches out to human beings in their different social and cultural environments and in the context created by their personal experiences. "Plurality in the church is the product and realization of Christ's love searching out each person in his or her proper identity."[1] Even in the diaspora, even when living

1. Werner Krusche, "Kirche in ideologischer Diaspora," *Kirche im Sozialismus* 1 (1974): 13.

19

in difficult political circumstances, the church does not demand uni-
formity of theological opinion. There are, Krusche continued, necessary
limits to intra-ecclesiastical pluralism, but what these limits are can only
be determined through patient theological conversation. Bishop
Krusche even suggested that the plurality-in-unity existing in the Protestant Church in the GDR, where the pluralism of ideas was prohibited,
was an evangelical sign.

Yet despite this pluralism, we find associated with the Kirchenbund the development of a theology that allowed the Christian community to reflect critically on the church's own past and draw important
lessons from it, to invent and evaluate new pastoral approaches and
policies, to react to initiatives taken by the government, and to respond
to the challenges of new historical situation. The Kirchenbund, founded
upon the consensus of eight regional churches — a consensus preserved
over the years, even in difficult times — was able to speak for the
Protestant Church in a single voice and make bold pastoral decisions
that were endorsed by all of its members.

The theology associated with the Bund allowed for a variety of
shades and emphases. It had its own internal plurality. Yet it always
preserved sufficient internal agreement to counsel united action and
produce consensus on matters of public importance. It also respected
the limits of what was acceptable to the churches.

Excluded by this consensus were in particular two theological
positions. The first one was the refusal on Christian grounds to
recognize the legitimacy of the East German state, seeing that it was
publicly committed to atheism. This was the position taken in the
fifties by Bishop Otto Dibelius, for whom the German Federal Republic (GFR) was the only legitimate Germany and the German
Democratic Republic (GDR) a godless episode destined soon to dis-
appear. While this view may have been shared by many Christians in
the fifties, an alternative viewpoint emerged in the same period, eventually to be accepted by the great majority, according to which the
GDR was the political state on Europe's geographical map where the
church was called upon to exercise its ministry. This matter — as we
shall see — was an important doctrinal issue for Lutherans since their
tradition, based on Romans 13, regarded obedience to the state as a
divine ordinance.

The second position excluded by the theological consensus was support for the ruling Communist party (SED) and surrender to its materialistic philosophy. This position was defended by a group of pastors, the Pfarrerbund, formed in 1954 and dissolved in 1974, which acknowledged Marxism-Leninism as verifiable scientific theory and hence acceptable to Christians as much as the natural sciences. This group interpreted Luther's doctrine of the two kingdoms in such a way that the Christian gospel, addressed to human hearts for their personal salvation, contained no relevant message for the realm of politics. The Christian Democratic Party (CDU) in East Germany, one of the so-called bloc parties, also gave unconditional support to the government. Over the years, this party tried to influence the Church's public policy, but the Church consistently declined.

The theology associated with the Bund was not uniform: it included currents of Christian thought that set the accents in different ways. But all the currents excluded both the rejection on principle of the GDR and the uncritical acceptance of the socialist state. "Neither total refusal nor total accommodation" became the Bund's theological motto.

The theology associated with the Bund had to deal with a much deeper source of disunity among its members. An historical fact I have not mentioned so far was that the eight regional churches federated in the Bund belonged to different doctrinal traditions. Three of the churches were strictly Lutheran: they belonged to the confessional union called VELK. Five of the churches were heirs of the Union of Lutherans and Reformed: their confessional union was called EKU.[2] The Lutheran churches, faithful to their tradition, were still unable to share the Eucharist with the Union churches. In addition to doctrinal disunity, the regional churches also had different cultural backgrounds: they represented regions that until the creation of Germany in 1870 had enjoyed their own social and political identity, an identity that had left its mark on the churches.

Yet there were several reasons why these churches wished to be more closely united. They shared a common faith, they recognized

2. For a more detailed account of these churches, see Robert Goeckel, *The Lutheran Church and the East German State: Political Conflict and Change under Ulbricht and Honecker* (Ithaca, NY: Cornell University Press, 1990), 15.

Christ's call to unity, they belonged to the same country, and they spoke the same language. They shared, moreover, the memory of an event of the recent past that was important to them. The Theological Declaration made by the Confessing Synod at Barmen in 1934, expressing resistance to Hitler's control of the church, had been signed by Lutherans and by churchmen of the Union. Barmen symbolized the possibility of church unity. Many years later, Bishop Johannes Hempel commented that "the unity experienced at Barmen under threatening conditions created a strong and enduring desire for a deeper ecclesiastical unity among the churches and their local congregations."[3]

Another reason for desiring greater unity was the new historical situation in the socialist society and the drastic drop in membership that accompanied it. To stand together, make joint pastoral decisions, and speak in a common voice was acquiring ever greater importance. There were even theologians who thought that the time of trial and the declining membership was a special occasion of grace, a chance given to the church to become a united community of disciples and thus regain an essential characteristic of Christian witness.[4]

While the Kirchenbund created in 1969 was not a church, it saw itself as more than a federation, as an ecclesiastical process through which the regional churches learned to think, act, and grow together in view of becoming a truly united church in the future.[5]

The effort of Europe's Lutheran and Reformed Churches after World War II to formulate a doctrinal consensus eventually produced the Leuenberg Concord in 1973. This ecclesiastical event further nourished the hope among the East German churches that their negotiations for structural unification would come to a successful conclusion. This was not to happen. Still, despite these ecclesiastical difficulties, the regional churches united in the Kirchenbund achieved a common understanding of what ministry, witness, and service meant

3. *Gemeinsam unterwegs. Dokumente aus der Arbeit des BEK in der DDR* (Berlin: Evangelische Verlagsanstalt, 1989), 202.

4. Albrecht Schönherr, *Horizont und Mitte. Aufsätze, Vorträge, Reden, 1953-1977* (München: Chr. Kaiser Verlag, 1979), 249.

5. See Article 1 of the Bund's founding document in Reinhard Henkys, *Bund der evangelischen Kirchen in der DDR. Dokumente zu seiner Entstehung* (Berlin: Eckart Verlag, 1970), 34.

in the GDR. The theology of the Kirchenbund — as we shall see — offered interpretations of the Lutheran doctrine of the two kingdoms and the Reformed doctrine of Christ's kingship that were respectful of both and showed them to be complementary. At the same time, the theology of the Bund preferred to formulate its understanding of the church's mission in society independently of these doctrines.

What I conclude from these reflections is that despite the pluralism within the East German Church, it is possible to speak of the theology (in the singular) associated with the Kirchenbund, a theology that enabled the Bund to make common pastoral decisions and address the church and the public in a single voice. This theology was not uniform; it existed with a variety of accents; but it was inspired by the same sources, sustained by the same historical memories, guided by the same vision, and capable of creating consensus in the church. This theology found articulation in the documents of the Synod, in the study commissions appointed by the Bund, and in a body of literature produced by bishops and theologians, consisting mainly of sermons, speeches, and articles. Getting permission for publishing books was not easy in the GDR.

The Church in East Germany did not produce theologians of high profile who acquired an international reputation.[6] Heino Falcke has argued that this was an advantage.[7] The important theological thinkers in East Germany thought of themselves not primarily as academics in conversation with their colleagues, but rather as pastors and intellectuals in dialogue with the churches and their local congregations. Best known among them were Heino Falcke, Günter Jacob, Werner Krusche, and Albrecht Schönherr. Their theology served proclamation and the church's ministry. Their theology, as we shall see, was contextual: it reflected the special conditions in the GDR. At the same time, because of close ties with the WCC, the Protestant theology in the GDR was also attentive to the global implications of the Christian message.

6. See Reinhard Stawinski, "Theologie in der DDR — DDR Theologie?" in *Die Evangelische Kirche in der DDR,* ed. Reinhard Henkys (München: Kaiser Verlag, 1982).

7. Heino Falcke, *Mit Gott Schritt halten. Reden und Aufsätze* (Berlin: Wichern-Verlag, 1986), 9.

Quite another question is how widely this theology was accepted by the members of the local congregations. Despite the repeated appeal to the laity to play a more active role in the church, Bishop Schönherr occasionally lamented that the church was still largely a Pfarrerkirche, a pastors' church, and that lay people in their day-to-day existence continued to be tempted by total withdrawal into private life or by external conformity to promote their careers.[8] At the same time, I have been impressed by written accounts recording the discussions and activities that took place in students' associations and in certain local congregations, suggesting a very active participation by lay people.[9] This is an issue for future research. Reflecting upon the rapid change of public opinion in society and the church after 1989, Bishop Werner Krusche mused that "the consensus in the church must have been smaller than we then thought."[10]

8. Albrecht Schönherr, *Abenteuer der Nachfolge. Reden und Aufsätze, 1978-1988* (Berlin: Wichern-Verlag, 1988), 146.

9. See Elisabeth Adler, "Freiheit in Grenzen: 40 Jahre Akademiearbeit in Berlin-Brandenburg," *Nachlese* [Berlin-Brandenburg: Evangelische Akademie] 1 (1992):1-32; Wolfgang Triebler, ed., *Die Erlöserkirche, Berlin-Lichtenberg, 1892-1992* (a book published by this congregation, 1992).

10. Werner Krusche, "Rückblick auf 21 Jahre Weg- und Arbeitsgemeinschaft im Bund der Evangelischen Kirchen" (Berlin: Sekretariat, Bund der Evangelischen Kirchen, 1991), 42.

CHAPTER 3

The Church's Pastoral Ministry

The foundation of the GDR created a new situation for the Christian church. Even if the Constitution of 1949 confirmed the freedom of religion and recognized the churches as public institutions, the majority of practicing Christians found it difficult to get used to the idea of living in a Communist state. Believing that the GDR was a dark cloud that would soon move away, they remained identified with West Germany, where the church was free, honored, and integrated into society.

While the Constitution of 1949 confirmed the rights the Protestant Church enjoyed during the Weimar Republic, including giving religious instruction within the school curriculum, the government, increasingly committed to Marxism-Leninism, began to use the school system to promote the official ideology and thus increasingly restricted the teaching of Christian doctrine. In the early years, the Church's appeal to the Constitution occasionally persuaded the government to make concessions. But after 1954, when West Germany entered the NATO Alliance, the situation changed. The Soviet Union created the Warsaw Pact, of which the GDR became a member. While the Eastern European nations recognized the GDR as a legitimate state, the West refused this recognition. According to the Hallstein doctrine, the German Federal Republic (GFR) was the only legitimate representative of Germany. In response, the GDR introduced the policy of delimitation (*Abgrenzung*) which sought to interrupt all contacts between East and

25

West German institutions, including the churches. Since the Protestant Church at that time tended to regard itself as the only bridge between the two Germanies, teaching Christian doctrine in the schools was suspected in the GDR as a political activity aimed at fostering the longing for an all-German unity. The government thus increased the pressure to marginalize religious instruction in the school system.

From the second half of the fifties on, a growing number of pastors and theologians questioned the church's yearning to restore the situation of the past and attachment to the memory of an undivided Germany. Some orthodox Lutherans, among them Bishop Moritz Mitzenheim, argued — appealing to Romans 13 — that secular authority was ultimately derived from God and that therefore the government of the GDR deserved the respect and obedience of its citizens.

Other theologians began to offer more daring theological reflections. In an article on this development, Hans-Jürgen Röder mentions three names in particular: Günter Jacob, Johannes Hamel, and Elisabeth Adler.[1] Günter Jacob, a theologian who held a high administrative position in the East German Church, delivered a controversial address, "Space for the Gospel in East and West," at the Synod of the EKD, the still united German Protestant Church, meeting at Berlin-Spandau in 1956. The church, Jacob set forth, faces the crucial decision whether to continue supporting and defending the Christendom idea, that is, society and culture determined by Christianity, or whether to recognize the theologically problematic character of the Constantinian era and distance itself from it in the name of the gospel. Jacob urged the church to resist the desire for restoration and abstain from any effort to regain the power and privileges of the past. What the church is held to do instead is to exercise its own proper mission. The church has a right to demand space in society: this is not a quest for power, but obedience to its mission to proclaim the gospel. Since political groups in the West were trying to use the Church (EKD) and its members in the GDR for their own purposes, Jacob urged the Church not to allow itself to become the rallying point of political reaction. Even though the Communist state, in keeping with its ideology, imposed unjust limits upon

---

1. Hans-Jürgen Röder, "Kirche im Sozialismus," in *Die Evangelische Kirche in der DDR,* ed. Reinhard Henkys (München: Kaiser Verlag, 1982), 62-85.

the Christian church, it did not thereby cease to be "authority" in the sense of Romans 13.[2]

In 1957 Johannes Hamel, in a widely distributed article, made an effort to persuade the local congregations to abandon their resentment-laden attitude toward their country and to find in their Christian faith support for a more constructive approach. A few years later, Elisabeth Adler, a leader in the Student Christian Movement, in a provocative piece, appealed to the church not to hibernate in the Communist society, not to withdraw and become sterile, but instead to seek contact, dialogue, and coresponsibility.

Günter Jacob's address at the Synod of 1956 also dealt with the Church's task to promote the Christian education of children attending atheist schools. This was a topic discussed by Jacob at other occasions.[3] According to him, the Protestant Church should strongly insist before the government that Christian parents have the right to send their children to schools where Christian teaching is not constantly contradicted. At the same time, he argued that to strengthen young people against atheistic philosophy they should be well informed about Marxism, and in particular take seriously the grain of truth in the Marxist critique of religion. The Church must teach that Christian life is not pious self-concern and withdrawal from social responsibility. The gospel properly understood summons the church to become a vital, interacting community dedicated to worship, public witness, and practical service in society. Jacob argued that religious instruction must change, abandon its focus on the individual, and recover a biblically based sense of community. Jacob's controversial speech was a signpost for the future orientation of the Protestant Church in the GDR.

Despite the Church's pleading with the government, the late fifties saw the complete exclusion of religious instruction from the public school system. The Church was thus forced to assume its own, independent responsibility for the Christian education of its children. This was not an easy undertaking. To fulfill this task the Church appointed

---

2. Pirkko Lehtiö, *Religionsunterricht ohne Schule. Die Entwicklung der Lage und des Inhaltes der evangelischen Christenlehre in der DDR von 1945-1959* (Münster: Comenius-Institut, 1983), 175.

3. Lehtiö, 176.

catechists, set up institutes to train them, assigned certain responsibility to local pastors, and, most importantly, mobilized the parents to involve themselves in the Christian education of their children. This process had many hurdles. What approach should such religious instruction take? Should it be taught as a subject in school as was done in the past? Or should the approach be more pastoral, focusing on the needs and concerns of the children? This question gave rise to important debates. Moreover, catechists and pastors, having been trained in different ways, did not always see eye to eye. In the local congregations the new approaches often created conflicts. Nor was it easy to involve the parents, who had never been trained to give religious instruction and whose commitment to the gospel was often lukewarm. Still, this was the way the Church had to go. Many years later, one of the achievements of the Kirchenbund was the development of a carefully elaborated program to help local congregations to assume the teaching responsibility for children and the young. Eventually Christian education became an important activity of the congregations, an evolution that gave them a new vitality and a sense of direction.

Moving the catechism from the school to the local congregation gave ordinary, church-going Christians the sense that the church was a living community, capable of responding creatively to a new situation. Christian education slowly became an enterprise involving the entire parish: it made the parents engaged and active members; it created a new sense of community; and it taught the parishioners how to articulate their faith. When, after the dissolution of the GDR in 1990, the Kirchenbund was devolved and the regional churches became again members of the EKD, bishops and pastors of the former GDR made a great effort, eventually unsuccessful, to keep the Christian education of children in the local congregation and not to return to the older German tradition, upheld in the GFR, that made Christian instruction a regular subject in school.

*   *   *

Despite many courageous voices, Christians at the end of the fifties and the beginning of the sixties were still divided in their attitude towards the new state. To illustrate this division, let me quote two texts produced in 1960, shortly before the erection of the Berlin Wall; one is taken from a hand-out distributed at a meeting of the (all-German) United Lutheran Church (VELK), and the other is a message addressed by the Union Church (EKU) to its members in the GDR.

> In the GDR the atheist worldview is the foundation of society and imposed in dictatorial fashion upon all citizens. The question arises whether Christians can live uprightly in this society at all. Christians are fulfilling their duties every day, but they are deeply burdened living in a state defined by a materialistic philosophy. The conflict between the religion of the state and the faith of Christians is taking on harsh and inescapable proportions as did the conflict at the time of Nero between the cult of the emperor and Christian faith.

> We give thanks to God that we stand under his divine rule in both parts of the country. . . . We give thanks to God that he inspired so many people to remain in the GDR at the place to which God had assigned them. Yet we also see with great concern how many people have left the GDR or remain in it against their will. Recognizing and taking seriously the pressing reasons for leaving, we have made a strong appeal to the government. But to our own congregations we call out: Thus says the Lord, "Fear not!" . . . We do not forget that in the GDR all citizens, the powerful and the powerless, are in the hand of the Risen One.[4]

In the sixties, the leading personalities in the Protestant Church gradually developed a clear sense that the GDR was their home, the location where God had placed them and where they were expected to exercise and prove their faith. Many of the East German church leaders had belonged to the Confessing Church under the Hitler regime: they regarded the fascist past of Germany as a great historical evil, looked upon the division of Germany as a just punishment, and tried to develop a sense of loyalty to the GDR as their own country. Some were even puzzled over why the West German government was willing to assign to high positions men whose past was heavily compromised by their role in Hitler's government.

4. Werner Krusche, "Rückblick auf 21 Jahre Weg- und Arbeitsgemeinschaft im Bund der Evangelischen Kirchen" (Berlin: Sekretariat, Bund der Evangelischen Kirchen, 1991), 28.

Albrecht Schönherr tells us of a learning experience that taught him to see himself as a responsible citizen of the GDR. In the late fifties, working as a pastor of a congregation near Potsdam, he was also responsible for the pastoral training of theological students.

> I discovered one day that the attitude I had to my society oriented toward socialism was largely determined by fear, stubbornness, and arrogance. I was reacting, rather than reflecting critically. Resisting Hitler's regime, I had developed a strong faith that there were no blank spots on God's geographical map. Yet what had happened to my faith since then! I decided to visit the civil servant responsible for church questions in the Postdam area and told him this: Please, be advised that I am a Christian and a pastor, not a partisan of the West. I stand here with both feet, but I stand here as a Christian.[5]

Bishop Werner Krusche recalled this:

> We came to look upon ourselves and act as citizens of the GDR. . . . What was developing among us was a sense of collective identity (*ein Wir-Gefühl*), almost impossible to explain, that came to the fore especially when people judged the GDR in an arrogant way.[6]

Experiences of this kind shared by many Christians gave rise to important theological reflections. Experience as starting point became a methodology frequently employed by the Protestant theology in GDR. The two theological themes that acquired great importance were discernment of place (*Ortsbestimmung*) and the learning process (*Lern-prozess*).

*   *   *

The emphasis on *Ortsbestimmung* or discernment of place meant to question Christians in the church who still dreamed of German unity and the privileged position enjoyed by the church in the past, and who

---

5. Albrecht Schönherr, *Abenteuer der Nachfolge. Reden und Aufsätze, 1978-1988* (Berlin: Wichern-Verlag, 1988), 42.
6. Werner Krusche, "Kritische Solidarität: der Weg der evangelischen Kirchen in der DDR," in *Theologische Studienabteilung* (Berlin: BEK, 1990), 6.

therefore refused to face the present situation and recognize the need to interpret anew the church's pastoral ministry. *Ortsbestimmung* implied a cultural-political analysis of the place where the church exercised its ministry, an analysis guided by the light of Christian faith.

Günter Jacob had already argued that the situation of Christians in the GDR called for new accents in the teaching of Christian doctrine. While Jesus Christ is the same yesterday, today, and forever, the proclamation of his message must take into account the historical conditions of the place. Pastors in the GDR recognized that it was highly problematic to go on teaching the Christian message in the GDR as they had learned it in the past, and as it was still being taught in West Germany. They felt that the emphasis on justification appeared to promote an inappropriate private or bourgeois consciousness among Christians and gave rise to false interpretations of the gospel by secular society. These pastors came to realize that while Christian teaching in Western society regarded itself as transcultural and universally valid, it was in actual fact — and quite unconsciously — contextual, reflecting the cultural conditions of its place in modern, bourgeois society.

In various parts of the GDR, ministers with a special pastoral concern formed friendship and study circles to discuss the meaning and power of the gospel in their country. Werner Krusche speaks with affection of the seminars and study groups in Lückendorf from which he drew his theological inspiration.[7] Albrecht Schönherr was closely associated with the Weissensee Study Circle in Berlin, which was to have considerable influence on the Protestant Church as a whole. In 1960, shortly before the erection of the Berlin Wall, Schönherr formulated six theses, which he submitted to the study circle for discussion. They reveal the inner wrestling going on among theologically oriented pastors and the gradual transformation of their consciousness. Here are the first three of these theses:

1. As our church encounters Marxism-Leninism in the inescapable form of state power, it is being radically transformed. We believe that we must accept this encounter as God's will. We must find

7. Werner Krusche, *Schritte und Markierungen. Aufsätze und Vorträge zum Weg der Kirche* (Berlin: Evangelische Verlagsanstallt, 1972), 10.

out how we, the congregation of Jesus Christ, can be obedient in this encounter. We hold that we must not look backwards to the traditions we have loved and the historical rights we had acquired; nor must we allow ourselves simply to react to the church's present difficulties and its declining membership or to the strategy of the Communists, thus allowing them to determine the logic of our action. We believe that we must look alone to the commission of Jesus Christ that has determined the life of his church from the very beginning (Matt. 28:18-20, Acts 1:8). We believe that we can discover in these troubled times God's guiding hand teaching us to become better witnesses for his cause.

2. We believe that the boundary between God's realm and the realm of Satan, between obedience and sin, is not identical with the boundaries of the Christian confessions, the world philosophies, and the spheres of power. Not theoretical atheism is the true danger for the church and the world, but the practical atheism of Christians, expressed in their fears, their quarrels, and their hypocrisy.

3. We believe that Christ has come because God has loved the world. God's aim is therefore not the church, but God's coming reign; not ecclesiastical existence, but the obedience of faith. God does not want a self-satisfied community in a ghetto, but witnesses who dare to move into the storm and render their passionate testimony even to atheists.[8]

This long quotation gives me the opportunity to make a brief remark on how a Catholic theologian like myself reacts to these powerful Protestant texts. I am amazed at how deeply the Lutheran "solus" is integrated into the German Protestant consciousness — *sola fide, sola scriptura, solus Christus.* The emerging contextual theology in the GDR is a reflection of this tradition. The three theses quoted above contain several expressions of the Lutheran "solus." The church, we are told, should not look back to the traditions of the past, but alone to the tradition recorded in the New Testament. The great

8. Albrecht Schönherr, *Horizont und Mitte. Aufsätze, Vorträge, Reden, 1953-1977* (München: Chr. Kaiser Verlag, 1979), 248.

danger for the church is not the cultural and political pressures exercised by atheists, but only the atheism or the absence of faith and love within the Christian community. God's redemptive action aims not at the church, but only at the world; and therefore the church should not wish to be the protected and beloved community, but define itself purely and simply through its mission in the world. Catholic theologians, as is well known — but not only Catholic theologians — would here insist on a qualifying "and." A point I wish to make throughout this study is that the Protestant theology in the GDR with its many "onlys" was nonetheless able to avoid one-sidedness and achieve great balance.

In a lecture given in 1962 to the theological faculty of Berlin's Humboldt University, Albrecht Schönherr offered a more systematic approach to the contextual theology that should guide the church's pastoral ministry.[9] The place of today's church is defined by two historical factors: first, the ever increasing industrialization of society, privileging a rational, secular approach to the world's problems; and second, related to this, the church's passage from its integration into society as a Volkskirche to a minority existence, a church in the diaspora. These two factors characterize the situation of the Protestant Church in both East and West Germany. In the GDR, the historical context is defined by an additional factor, the encounter — for the first time in history — of a large Reformation church with Marxism-Leninism in the inescapable form of state power. The attempt to avoid this encounter, Schönherr continued, would not only be unrealistic, but would betray the church's call and mission. He added, "Petitionary prayers for the governing authorities, commanded by Scripture (1 Tim. 2:1), are appropriate only when they are based on a critical understanding of these powers." Students, he argued, could not think theologically and engage in pastoral ministry unless they made an *Ortsbestimmung*, acquainted themselves with the dominant ideology, listened to it with theological ears, and then tried to express the meaning and power of the gospel in the socialist society.

This new pastoral approach received growing support. In 1963 the leadership conference of the Protestant churches published "Ten

9. Schönherr, *Horizont und Mitte*, 91-92.

Articles on the Church's Freedom and Service" (mentioned in chapter 1) that reflected the new orientation. We have already quoted above the following brief excerpt:

> In existing social conditions we must ascertain what God wants from us and do good according to his will. We fall prey to a lack of faith if we assume that God has abandoned us in the existing conditions and thus begin to doubt, or if we interpret the historical and social circumstances as the direct gift of the will of God and accept them without reservation.[10]

*   *   *

Pastoral theology based on *Ortsbestimmung* eventually led the Protestant churches to create the Kirchenbund in 1969. We saw in chapter 1 that there were political and strategic reasons for setting up an East German church federation in relative independence from the West German EKD. The point I wish to make in this chapter is that there were also urgent pastoral reasons for this. "It is simply not true," writes Bishop Krusche, "that the formation of the Bund was simply due to the situation created by the new Constitution of 1968 and therefore the result of political pressure." There was an "inner reason," he continued, why the Bund was created, namely theological and pastoral necessity.[11]

The Kirchenbund brought together the eight regional churches in a community defined by a common pastoral concern. The founding document, the Ordnung, invoked the Barmen Declaration of 1934, a previous occasion when Protestants of different regional churches expressed their joint pastoral commitment (Art. 1,3). At present, though the regional churches retained their autonomy, the Kirchenbund was more than a simple federation: it defined itself as a institutional process by which the churches "deepened their cooperation" and "grew together" so as to think and act as one Christian community (Art. 1,1

10. Robert Goeckel, *The Lutheran Church and the East German State: Political Conflict and Change under Ulbricht and Honecker* (Ithaca, NY: Cornell University Press, 1990), 63.
11. Krusche, "Rückblick auf 21 Jahre Weg," 9.

and 1,2).[12] The Bund thought of itself as a church in the making. In its relations *ad extra,* for instance in addressing the government or participating in the ecumenical movement, it presented itself as the Protestant Church of the GDR. *Ad intra,* by contrast, the Kirchenbund respected the diversity of the federated churches, relied on their approval, and followed the collective decisions made by them at the yearly Synod. The multiple activities of the Bund were directed by an executive committee — with Schönherr as first president — elected by the Synod and responsible to it.

Bishop Schönherr, gifted thinker and political actor, was able to preserve and strengthen the unity of Kirchenbund, even in difficult situations, despite its internal pluralism. He has rightly been called a *Kirchenvater* of the East German Church. Even when he and his executive committee engaged in bold negotiations with Erich Honecker on March 6, 1978, the federated churches, despite their differing emphases, supported and endorsed the agreement at the subsequent Synod. This unity of the Bund, preserved throughout history, allows us to say that associated with it was a theology — a theology in the singular.

Neither federation nor Church in the strict sense, the Bund constituted itself as "a community of witness and service" (*eine Zeugnis- und Dienstgemeinschaft).* These three words — community, witness, and service — had a profound and innovative meaning for the participants. They offered a contextual ecclesiology. They presented an understanding of the church and its pastoral ministry that was gained after the *Ortsbestimmung.*

Defining itself as a *community,* the Bund saw itself as an agent that led Christians of the GDR into conversation and cooperation, rescued them from their inherited isolation, urged them to abandon individualistic piety and withdrawal, and fostered a pastoral approach that sought to create fellowship in the local congregations and enabled them to assume collective responsibility in their society.

Witness was here defined as "word and deed announcing the truth of Christ in the world." The Church here saw itself as a

---

12. The nature of the Bund is defined in Article 1 of its Ordnung, its founding document. See Reinhard Henkys, *Bund der evangelischen Kirchen in der DDR. Dokumente zu seiner Entstehung* (Berlin: Eckart Verlag, 1970), 34.

missionary community. Its concern was not self-preservation and institutional security, but giving effective testimony to Christ in the GDR. This did not mean that the Church thought its principal task was to oppose and refute the officially imposed atheism. To give testimony to Christ demanded that Christians first listen to their society, understand its aspirations and its problems, and then communicate — in word and deed — the meaning of the gospel in their historical situation. The Church's witness thus contextually determined had a political dimension.

Service or *diakonia* was defined as the effort of the Church — speaking and acting — to help people in need and make more just the society to which it belonged. The Church here saw Christian faith as a praxis, as discipleship, as an obedience to God that included solidarity with people at the margin, especially the poor and oppressed.

The character of the Bund as community of witness and service continued to be discussed by the member churches. When the churches achieved greater doctrinal consensus, especially after the Leuenberg Concord, they wanted to express this greater unity in the foundational document of the Bund; and yet in fidelity to the remaining differences, they did not want this document to exaggerate the existing unity.[13] In 1985 a new text confirmed the unity of the Church's pastoral ministry:

> Because God's Word is intended for all human beings, the Protestant Church is committed to give witness to it, publicly and to everyone. It thus sees the society in which it lives as the God-given place where to express its faith, hope, and love. With the freedom discovered in the obedience to God's Word, the Church accepts its responsibility for the life of society. It supports the efforts of Christians to cooperate with people of other convictions, fostering human well-being, justice, and peace. In this, special attention is given to people suffering deprivation and people urged against their conscience.[14]

It is interesting that in the seventies, the Bund began to realize that an exclusive emphasis on witness and service made an excessive

13. *Gemeinsam unterwegs. Dokumente aus der Arbeit des BEK in der DDR* (Berlin: Evangelische Verlagsanstalt, 1989), 31-42.
14. *Gemeinsam,* 42.

demand on the local congregations and did not respect the problems ordinary Christians experienced in their lives. Especially Christians in small congregations felt that the Kirchenbund was not speaking to them at all. The Bund — always willing to learn — developed an extensive pastoral program that supported and affirmed the parishioners and provided biblical and critical education for them. Congregations needed personal pastoral care if they were to give public witness and serve the wider society. The pedagogues of the Kirchenbund turned to psychological studies made in the West to create a program that would help pastors and church workers to accompany people in the different phases of their lives — childhood, youth, adulthood, and old age — always paying attention to the special conditions created by their personal histories.[15] Here, as at many other occasions, the theology of the Kirchenbund revealed that despite its boldness, it sought to avoid one-sidedness and find a proper balance.

*   *   *

The Protestant Church had to learn new ways. Since the bishops and pastors who created the Kirchenbund and continued to shape its policies were involved in a learning process, a process often involving the pain of unlearning inherited attitudes, they realized that the entire Church, including the local congregations, had to become a learning community.

Bishop Schönherr put great emphasis on the Church as a learning community. Since he was conscious of the learning he had undergone in his faith, he realized that believers could not assimilate a new perspective unless they were willing to be challenged by the new and raise uncomfortable questions regarding their inheritance. Learning was here not simply the acquisition of new skills or the assimilation of new concepts: learning involved the transformation of faith consciousness. Learning took place within faith. Ultimately, learning occurred through listening to God's revealed Word in a new historical situation.

15. Roland Degen, *Gemeindeerneuerung als gemeinpädagogische Aufgabe* (Münster/Berlin: Comenius-Institut, 1992), 73-82, 120-145.

Schönherr presented a theology of learning based on biblical teaching.[16] Jesus himself was a teacher. What he taught was both in continuity
and discontinuity with past teaching. He challenged his listeners with a
new message that was seemingly at odds with the ideas they had received,
but that upon reflection revealed itself as faithful to the best of their
tradition. The teaching of Jesus did not communicate information, but
it was rather a message that transformed people's awareness and their lives.
In this sense, believers were learners. Schönherr mentioned that when
Luther translated the Greek word for "disciple" by the German word
Jünger, he left the readers unaware that the disciples of Jesus were pupils
or learners. Discipleship — in German, *Nachfolge* — included the readiness to learn. Faith was accompanied by learning.

The apostles remained learners. Moving from preaching the gospel
to the Jews to preaching it to the Gentiles was a painful and controversial process in which Paul took the lead and challenged the other
apostles to follow his example. With the apostles, the entire church of
Jerusalem had to become a learning community. Even after these events,
Schönherr argued, Paul remained a learner. "I press on to make it [the
knowledge of Christ and his power] my own, because Christ Jesus has
made me his own. Beloved, I do not consider that I have made it my
own; but this one thing I do: forgetting what lies behind and straining
forward to what lies ahead, I press on" (Phil. 3:12-14, NRSV). The
learning process has no end in the life of the church.

Yet the biblical message, Schönherr insisted, is not a set of principles that must be accepted and obeyed. What the message announces
are the *mirabilia Dei,* the marvellous things that God has done for our
salvation, culminating in the historical mission of Jesus Christ. Jesus,
and after him the apostles, explained what these events meant and what
actions they called for in the particular conditions of their time and
place. Because Luther still lived in an agrarian, patriarchal, and highly
stratified society, not so far removed from the biblical world, he thought
that the message of the New Testament was easy to understand and to
apply in daily practice. He and his followers were learners, because in
reliance on the clear message of the gospel, they left behind the practice
in which they were brought up and entered upon a new way. But,

16. Schönherr, *Horizont und Mitte,* 206-227.

Schönherr argued, modern society has become so different that learning what the gospel summons us to do has become very difficult, especially in the GDR where a new situation demands that Christians unlearn what they have inherited from the days when the Protestant Church enjoyed social status and power. In the GDR, the Church must become a community learning to follow on a new path.

Newness of this kind, Schönherr continued, cannot be put into words by church leaders and their synods and passed on in an authoritative, unquestioning way to the wider church community. The new direction cannot be assimilated simply by submitting to it. Christians in their parishes must be willing to experience the challenge, question their past, detach themselves from inherited patterns, and listen anew to God's Word in Scripture. It is in this highly personal learning process that the Kirchenbund wanted to be helpful to Christians in their local congregations. This was the purpose of the Synod of 1974 on the theme of "The Church as a Learning Community."

Churches teach, but they also learn. To illustrate this principle Schönherr, addressing the 1974 Synod, referred to the learning experience of the Catholic Church at the Vatican Council II in the early sixties. As a Catholic theologian, I wish to add here that while the bishops at the Council underwent a profound learning experience, they did not ask themselves the theological question of how the results of the Council, the new way, could be communicated to the regional churches and the local congregations. The Catholic bishops and the Pope believed without much reflection that the new way could be introduced by an appeal to ecclesiastical authority. They uncritically supposed that learning within the faith was the same as assimilating authoritative information. The absence of an appropriate theology limited the impact of the Vatican Council on the Catholic Church.

The Protestant Church in the GDR clearly recognized that the learning process must engage Christians personally and involve their local congregations. There is, however, a certain ambiguity in Schönherr's lectures in regard to *who* teaches the church. From whom does the church learn?

On the one hand, Schönherr emphasizes that the church learns from God's Word alone. The world is not competent to teach the church. Divine revelation summed up once and for all in Jesus Christ is the church's sole teacher. The world raises issues, sometimes urgent ones, from which the church may not run away, but learning within faith takes place as Christians, with these issues in mind, reread the Scriptures, reflect on God's Word, and hear the gospel in a new way. The entire learning process is due to the divine initiative, since it is God who touches the heart, questions the deep, shakes the sense of the taken-for-granted, and enables believers to detach themselves from inherited ideas and respond in newness to the burning issues of the time. In this process, Christians may accept ideas derived from secular sources, but only if they can be verified and confirmed by the Scriptures.

In 1978 Schönherr gave a lecture in Munich on the church as a learning community.[17] The Protestant Church in the GDR, Schönherr explained to the West German audience, interprets its historical situation as the school to which God is sending it. Christians first learned to discern their place and then how to proclaim the gospel in witness and service to their society. In faith the Church affirms its presence in the GDR. This does not mean, he added, that the Church has opted for Communism, but it does mean that the Church has opted for the people who must live their lives in a communist society. Schönherr quoted the declaration from the Synod of 1973 that "the Church must help the Christian citizens and their local congregations to live their lives in a socialist society in the freedom and bondage of faith and to make every effort to promote the best for all and for society as a whole."[18] We bear the torch, he said, into an as yet untraveled territory, but we trust in God, who faithfully continues to teach us.

Trust in God drives out fear. Schönherr told his audience of a meeting with Hans Steigewasser, the state secretary for church questions, at which the church leaders expressed their worry about the impending new constitution. Steigewasser asked the bishops, "Are you afraid of the future?" Schönherr commented: "Such a question from the mouth of a Marxist one does not forget! But what was so special about this question? In Lutheran spirituality, with its emphasis on trusting God alone, the fear of the future, it would seem, is the sign of a waning faith. Believing in God means to be delivered from anxiety."

17. Schönherr, *Abenteuer,* 41-55.
18. Schönherr, *Abenteuer,* 42.

On the other hand, we also hear from Schönherr that the church must learn from others, in particular from Marxists. He takes up in greater detail the suggestion first made by Günter Jacob in 1956 that to keep the Christian faith and give public witness to it in the GDR, it is necessary to understand and take seriously the Marxist critique of religion. Schönherr mentions six issues important for theology and the church's ministry that demand that the church listen to Marxist-Leninist thought and critically learn from it.[19]

First, Schönherr is impressed by the Marxist view of praxis. Not only does theory here follow upon practice, but according to this view, the truth of theory must be tested by practice. Sharing a consensus among praxis-theologians in other parts of the world, Schönherr finds that this idea helps theologians to recognize — as they had not done in the past — that biblical faith itself is a praxis, grounded in surrender to God's Word and tested by practice. To test whether the church remains faithful to the gospel, one must not only look at what the church proclaims, but also examine what the church does and what impact the church's teaching has on society.

Second, the Marxist perspective reveals that whatever is personal and private is conditioned by its social context and cannot be truly understood unless this social relationship has been uncovered. Christians must ask themselves whether their highly personal understanding of justification has not painted a false picture of the human condition and promoted a harmful individualism in Western society. Historical conditions that Christians now deplore may be due in part to the church's own sins. Schönherr alludes here to the pious withdrawal from society, accompanied by unquestioning outer conformity to it, that has characterized much of Christian history, including in particular the Lutheran tradition.

Third, Marxist philosophy sees the human being as an ensemble of social relations. We may reply to this that humans are more than focal points in the web of human interaction because God has created them as responsible subjects. They have souls. Yet we must also be willing to recognize that traditional Protestant theology tended to understand human beings as unrelated individuals. Was the primacy

19. Schönherr, *Horizont und Mitte*, 221-222.

assigned to preaching over communal liturgical practice based on such a narrow view? Listening to the Marxist critique of the bourgeois concept of the individual, the church gains a clearer sense that its pastoral ministry must aim at the creation of believing communities through the common reading of the Bible, dialogue, worship, and concerted action.

Fourth, Marxist philosophy reveals that economic and political powers play a decisive role in the course of human history. Christians must ask themselves, therefore, whether there can be an obedience of faith, a faithful surrender to God's Word, that is unrelated to these worldly powers and excludes social and political solidarity.

Fifth, Marxists see religion as an anesthetic for the exploited lower classes. This prompts Christians to ask whether the church has not often defended unjust political systems and offered to the poor the consolation of eternal life. Rereading the Scriptures in the present, Christians have discovered that the gospel summons and empowers them to assume responsibility for their world.

Sixth, the government of the GDR offered support to colonized and exploited nations in their struggle for liberation. Instead of searching for the ideological motives behind this policy, Christians should ask themselves whether they should not extend their solidarity to the poor and oppressed and become the church for others.

Schönherr also interpreted as a challenge to Christians the passion and determination of the Communist government to implement what it regarded as the liberating truth. Do we have the same sense of mission? he asked. Do we have the same commitment?

These are examples where the church listens to others, studies their writings, examines their actions and learns from them. Schönherr wanted to combine this critical openness to the world with the Protestant (especially Barthian) affirmation mentioned above that the church is suspicious of all human wisdom and relies on God's Word alone. For many Lutherans, reason is competent in the worldly world, but has little to say in the sphere of salvation. Schönherr favored greater openness. He thought that the church can and should learn insights from others if these insights stand up under the test of Scripture. Christians learn from their encounter with Marxism, Schönherr proposed, what they should have known all along from reading the Bible.[20] But is this a sufficient reply to the question? Schönherr does not explore in depth the relationship between learning from God and learning from humans. It is my impression that Schönherr, and with him the theology of the Kirchenbund, has learned something about the human condition from the Marxist version of the Enlightenment tradition that as such is not found in the Scriptures.

Whether or not this theological question has been adequately resolved, the Protestant Church in the GDR saw itself as a learning community. It even learned from its own experiences, following the method of trial and error. Often when the church leadership called for resistance against government policies that demanded a sacrifice, for instance the refusal to participate in the youth dedication ceremony (Jugendweihe), the majority of Christians expressed their reluctance. In this particular case, parents did not want their children to be excluded from higher education. The Church learned from these experiences, according to Bishop Krusche, where to push the government and where to go easy.[21]

The church as learning community became a central concept in the East German Protestant theology. The Church even proposed to the GDR government that it too should understand itself as a learning community, becoming more open to the perspective of others. In his address to the Synod of 1978, explaining the significance of the agreement with Erich Honecker on March 6, Schönherr invoked the universal importance of learning:

> The meeting of March 6 was the result of a long and sometimes painful learning process for all participants. To this learning process have contributed not only the experiences of Christians and Marxists, who discovered forty years ago in their resistance to fascist inhumanity that what they held in common was greater and more enduring than what their differences made them expect, but also the necessary cooperation between Christians and Marxists in some sectors of society from the very beginning facilitated a certain mutual understanding that could not have been anticipated, knowing the differ-

20. Schönherr, *Abenteuer,* 54.
21. Werner Krusche, "6 März: 1978-1988 ein Lernweg" (Berlin: Sekretariat, Bund der Evangelischen Kirchen, 1988), 9.

ence between the two traditions. This learning process must continue. Where the issue is greater peace and greater justice, where help is offered to people suffering from deprivation or persecution, where the social relations between us is being improved, there Christians will cooperate and in turn receive encouragement. Yet the Protestant Church's presence as church . . . makes it impossible that it ever become a socialist renewal committee. For the Church is and remains, first and last, the church of the one Lord Jesus Christ.[22]

22. Schönherr, *Abenteuer,* 52.

CHAPTER 4

The Spirit of Stuttgart and Darmstadt

The leadership of the churches in the GDR was for the most part in the hands of men who had been members of the Confessing Church. They had resisted the control Hitler imposed upon the church, and the memory of their struggle continued to be a source of inspiration in their theological reflections. The Barmen Declaration of 1934, signed by Lutheran, Reformed, and United Christians, remained an authoritative document for the Kirchenbund, cited in its Ordnung, its founding document. For these Christians, the Protestant motto, *ex tenebris ad lucem,* acquired a new and haunting meaning.

This orientation had a certain affinity with the public philosophy of the GDR. The Communist state saw itself as the victorious creation after a long and painful antifascist struggle. In the twenties, German Communists tried to gain power and transform their country; in the thirties they were beaten, tortured, and killed in Hitler's concentration camps; but in the forties, the Soviet Union succeeded, after enormous sacrifices, in defeating Hitler's Germany and subsequently allowed German Communists to create their own state. Over the years the GDR continued to define itself as an antifascist society. The Communists had their own interpretation of *ex tenebris ad lucem.* In the GDR, the 8th of May, the day of the German collapse under the Allies' successful invasion, was celebrated every year as the Day of Liberation.

For the Protestant Church, the German past raised the painful theological questions of German guilt, the Church's complicity, and

the contemporary meaning of forgiveness. After years of political reflection and spiritual wrestling, the leaders of the Church in the GDR
adopted the position that Germany had produced the Nazi phenomenon, started the war, organized the mass murder of the Jews, killed
several millions of other people, was finally defeated, and — as its
punishment — split into two parts. This punishment, they held, was
well-deserved: Christians had no reason to complain or to remain
sentimentally attached to a united Germany. This sense of German
guilt helped many Christians to accept living in a Communist society
as their divinely-appointed lot, as the place where they were called to
serve God's purposes, and eventually as the country they willingly called
their *Heimat,* their home.

Albrecht Schönherr has treated the question of guilt and the
practical meaning of forgiveness in some detail. His writings reveal
that the declarations of guilt made after the Second World War by
Christian leaders in the EKD, at Stuttgart and later at Darmstadt,
were influential documents repeatedly invoked by the Kirchenbund
in the GDR.[1]

Immediately after the war, at an ecumenical meeting held at
Stuttgart in October 1945, the Protestant Church published a controversial statement confessing its guilt in the German catastrophe. How
did this come about? The worldwide ecumenical community was eager
for an international reconciliation of the Christian churches. The initiative was taken by W. A. Visser 't Hooft, the respected ecumenical
spokesman from Holland, who was later to become the first general
secretary of the WCC. Joined by other ecumenical personalities from
countries that had defeated Germany, Visser 't Hooft invited the German Protestant Church to a meeting to be held at Stuttgart in October
1945. To make Christian reconciliation possible, the international
churchmen asked the German Church to make a public statement
admitting German guilt and confessing the Church's complicity in
Hitler's reign of death.

---

1. Albrecht Schönherr, *Horizont und Mitte. Aufsätze, Vorträge, Reden, 1953-1977*
(München: Chr. Kaiser Verlag, 1979), 260-269; Schönherr, *Abenteuer der Nachfolge.
Reden und Aufsätze, 1978-1988* (Berlin: Wichern-Verlag, 1988), 92-102, 149-173,
190-198. Subsequent references to *Abenteuer* will be made parenthetically in the text.

At an earlier meeting in August 1945, which laid the foundation for a united Protestant Church (EKD), Martin Niemöller had already urged the Church to make a public confession of its guilt. But his message was not heard at that time. At Stuttgart, upon the invitation of the ecumenical community, the German churchmen decided to compose such a declaration, though they had not been prepared for it. This is the first paragraph:

> We are grateful for this ecumenical visit because we see ourselves united with our people not only in a community of suffering, but also in the solidarity of guilt. With great pain we say: Through us has come endless suffering over many peoples and their countries. What we have often told our local congregations, we now pronounce in the name of the entire Church: In the name of Jesus Christ we have struggled over many years against the spirit that found a frightening expression in the national-socialist dictatorship, yet we accuse ourselves of not having confessed more courageously, prayed more faithfully, believed more cheerfully, and loved more passionately. (Schönherr, *Abenteuer,* 94)

The declaration continued, "Now a new beginning shall be made in our churches."

Stuttgart was not well received by Christians in Germany. Many of them, including some bishops and theologians, felt that Germany's and the church's guilt could only be acknowledged in a statement that also pointed to the guilt of Germany's enemies. By contrast, Christians who had stood firmly against the Nazi regime in the past found the Stuttgart declaration vague, lacking in candor and incisiveness.

These Christians welcomed the sentence, "With great pain we say: through us has come endless suffering over many peoples and their countries." For them, this was the true spirit of Stuttgart. Yet they were aware that this sentence, inserted in the text only upon Niemöller's urging, failed to be connected with the rest of the declaration. That the Protestant Church as a whole had wrestled against the spirit of fascism, Schönherr insisted, was simply not true. Even the Confessing Church, a minority in Germany, had only opposed Hitler's interference in the Church's autonomy; and apart from some of its members, refused to make a political statement against Nazi theory and practice. To describe the complicity of the Church simply as not having confessed, prayed, believed, and loved strongly enough, disguised rather than revealed the truth. And finally, the call for "a new beginning" was not accompanied by any concrete plan.

Karl Barth, supported by theologians such as Niemöller and Iwand, urged Christians in Germany to express the spirit of Stuttgart in a more detailed declaration. Barth's writings in the thirties on "political worship" (*politischer Gottesdienst*), that is, the worship of God implicit in the Christian struggle against social evil, acquired a new meaning for a group of churchmen, formerly members of the Confessing Church, who now constituted themselves as a "Bruderrat," a council of brothers. They complained that the EKD was unwilling to learn from the Church's failure in the past, and instead of using the postwar conditions to make "a new beginning," was actually returning to the old bureaucratic spirit. The postwar Church, the Bruderrat lamented, refused to discuss the meaning and power of the gospel for the German people in these troubled times. The Bruderrat held a meeting at Darmstadt in 1947, at which the members formulated seven theses addressed to the German Church. Several years later, the message of Darmstadt influenced the Protestant theology in the GDR.

According to Darmstadt, the message that Christ has reconciled the world with God cannot be heard and received by us, Christians of Germany, unless we readily confess our fathers' and our own transgressions. These transgressions culminated in the evil period of the Nazi regime when, through us, endless suffering came upon millions of people and their lands. But we had already gone astray in the nineteenth century when we dreamed of a special German mission as if German genius was able to resolve the world's problems. Such dreams prepared us for the unlimited use of political power and placed our nation on the throne of God. We went astray when we mobilized Christian resistance against progressive social change and supported conservative forces that protected the traditional ways at any price — this was an allusion to the spiritual identification of the German Protestant Church with the Prussian monarchy, later the German empire. We denied the people the right to revolution, but we tolerated or even approved the arrival of dictatorship. We erred when we believed that the clash between good and evil could be resolved by the use of political power. We went astray when we failed to recognize that Marxist economic materialism offered a warning to the Church that it not forget the this-worldly side of its mission, to serve the earthly well-being of the human family. "We refrained from making the just cause of the poor and disenfranchised the cause of Christianity, in obedience to the gospel of God's coming reign" (Schönherr, *Abenteuer,* 196).

The positive message of Darmstadt was that, having confessed their sins, Christians in Germany were now freed by the grace of Christ to exercise their ministry in a new, more faithful way, worshipping God and serving the spiritual and material well-being of humankind. Christians were now freed from their entanglement with Western culture and empowered to extend their solidarity to peoples everywhere and to become agents of peace and understanding on the international level.

The Darmstadt declaration produced a storm of indignation among Christians in Germany. It did not receive the endorsement of the Protestant Church (EKD). A few years later, Gustav Heinemann said: "The [German] people were unwilling to accept the Stuttgart declaration. . . . Even the churches, apart from the openness of some of their members, reacted to it with incomprehension and repudiation. Thus our own experience of hubris and catastrophe, of judgment and divine grace, did not on the whole become an occasion for a conversion and a new beginning" (Schönherr, *Abenteuer,* 99). Many years later, Bishop Werner Krusche, speaking in the GDR, frankly admitted that "the Protestant Church, out of a false understanding of pastoral care and the fear of losing its reputation before the nation, shifted the attention from its own guilt to that of others, and thereby cheated itself and the entire people of a chance for a truly new beginning after the war" (Schönherr, *Abenteuer,* 193).

Another important ecclesiastical expression of the spirit of Stuttgart and Darmstadt occurred in 1962 when the EKD published a position paper in the German Federal Republic (GFR), the so-called *Ostdenkschrift,* on the need for a new relationship of Germany with Poland and other nations that Germany had invaded. This was an important but delicate issue. Poland was rightly afraid that the Germans would not accept the new Polish-German border, cutting off, as it did, large regions that had been German for centuries. At the same time, the German government in Bonn, under pressure from angry Germans exiled from the eastern regions, was unwilling to make any promises to Poland. The Church Commission for Social Responsibility, appointed by the EKD, approached the issue in the spirit of Stuttgart and Darmstadt, recognizing Germany's guilt, the need for repentance, the readiness to make reparation, and the importance of eventual reconciliation. Because of strong protest among the local congregations, the EKD accepted the position paper only somewhat half-heartedly, even if on the political level the paper turned out to be the starting point for a change in Germany's official relationship to Poland.[2]

The spirit of Stuttgart and Darmstadt inspired the churchmen in the GDR who created the Kirchenbund. Already in 1956 Günter Jacob had declared that the Church must accept the end of the Constantinian era and be ready to live as a minority without its privileges and the support of the state. Several years later, a spiritual conversion enabled church leaders to define the Kirchenbund as "a community of witness and service." The church obedient to God's Word was to serve the human community and offer support to the poor and the weak. The Protestant Church began to define itself as the church-for-others. The spirit of Stuttgart and Darmstadt was present when the Kirchenbund publicly regretted the Church's former association with the Prussian monarchy and its military tradition, and defined its role in society as a servant of peace and a proponent of nonviolence. The same spirit was present when Bishop Schönherr declared that among those who actively opposed the Hitler regime the great majority were Communists, often sacrificing their own lives. The Kirchenbund believed that its new, bold ecclesiology was not only supported by a network of radicals, but upheld by Christians in the local congregations.

The spirit of Stuttgart and Darmstadt also defined the Church's relationship to the Jewish community in the GDR. The Church preached a message of repentance, restitution, and reconciliation. Bishops and pastors commemorated the 9th of November, 1938, the night of a nation-wide pogrom against the German Jews, when synagogues burned in every German city, sign and symbol of the horror that was

2. See Gregory Baum, "The Role of the Churches in German-Polish Reconciliation," in *The Reconciliation of Peoples: Challenge to the Churches*, ed. Gregory Baum and Harold Wells (Maryknoll, NY: Orbis, forthcoming).

to come. On November 9, 1973, Bishop Schönherr addressed the Jewish community in Berlin (East):

> The night of the broken glass on November 9, 1938, was a culminating point of the persecution inflicted on the Jews in the "Third Reich." Apparently the Nazi regime wanted to test how far it could go. . . . The people neither interfered with the SA [Hitler's paramilitary troops], nor did they respond to the pogrom allowing it to have the support of the masses. The Nazi regime drew its conclusion from this: all subsequent persecution would have to happen in secret. Yet even the planned extermination of the Jews would not arouse the people to serious resistance. On the burning of the synagogues thus followed the fire of the death chambers in the extermination camps. It would have been the duty of Christians not to remain inactive. Yet protest and outrage were heard from very few pulpits. Many Christians shook their heads, but very few took any risks. The church struggle of the Confessing Church began when pastors of Jewish ancestry were being dismissed. But for the other Jews, only very few did something; the official ecclesiastical leadership did nothing at all. . . . Commemorating the 9th of November will always summon Christians to ask for forgiveness. Seeing the poor, helpless, tormented, persecuted neighbor, we walked by. (Schönherr, *Abenteuer*, 90)

Bishop Schönherr repeatedly explained that the struggle of the Confessing Church sought to protect the autonomy of the Church, not to offer political resistance to the fascist regime. One leadership group did produce a document in 1936 that defended the Church's freedom and also repudiated the hate propaganda against the Jews, the racist policies of the government, the activities of the secret police, and the institution of concentration camps. Yet this paper remained a secret; when its content was later revealed by indiscretion, the authors regretted having composed it. The one exception was the message of the Confessing Synod at Breslau in 1944 that condemned the mass murder of the Jews (Schönherr, *Abenteuer*, 95). Yet on the whole, the Church did not express political opposition against the Hitler regime, even though in a totalitarian state any critical word has a destabilizing effect.

The Kirchenbund, especially through the voice of its president, Bishop Schönherr, would not allow the GDR to forget the mass murder of the Jews. On the 9th of November, 1978, Schönherr spoke at the ruins of the synagogue in Berlin's Oranienburger Strasse, a synagogue that has since been restored. His theme at that time was "It all began when someone said, 'the Jew,' 'the Pole,' 'the Communist'; and it ended in Auschwitz" (Schönherr, *Abenteuer,* 106). After recalling the great horror, he vowed "before this desecrated house of God" that we will never respect other people less than ourselves because they are different, have a different skin color, different convictions, different religious beliefs, a different lifestyle, a different gender, or a different upbringing.

The destruction of Dresden by the British Airforce on February 13, 1945, killed hundreds of thousands of citizens. Every year the day is commemorated in Dresden. In 1983 when Bishop Schönherr was invited to address a Christian congregation in that city, he said,

> Thirty-eight years ago Dresden was burning. Dresden — the burning Dresden — like Coventry, like Leningrad, like Hiroshima, is a deep wound in the body of humankind that has not yet healed. But the fire of Dresden was not the first. On the 9th of November, 1938, the synagogues burnt everywhere in the German Reich. (Schönherr, *Abenteuer,* 127)

At this occasion, when people came to mourn their own relatives burnt to death, Schönherr had the courage to retell the story of the fires set by Germans and later set by others that preceded the conflagration of Dresden. Again he dealt with the question of how Christians could have been so blind that they did not see the evil when the first clear signs appeared. The boycott of Jewish stores on April 1, 1933, was not read by them as a warning of what was to come. When new laws were made excluding Jews from their rights as citizens, the Church had nothing to say. Christians did not allow themselves to be warned because they were too attached to the economic upswing and the national honor and too stupid to see through the clever propaganda in which Hitler, invoking "the Almighty" and "divine Providence," related his political aims to the Christian vision. In this context Schönherr mentioned the names of the martyrs and heros, Protestant and Catholic, who helped the Jews, resisted the fascist government and, in most instances, paid with their lives for their acts of love. But the majority of Christians, even though not convinced National-Socialists, remained silent till the very end. Why? Because depending on the official news and propaganda, they knew too little; because having inherited a certain Lutheran contempt for political involvement, they had no practice in making up their own minds; and because of the cruelty and terror of the Hitler regime, they were simply afraid.

> They told us that we were a master race (*Herrenvolk*), while the others, especially the Slavic people, were meant to be our slaves. What kind of master race were we! A people of low-brow conformists (*Spiesser*) subservient to those in power and arrogant in our public posturing, standing with legs apart like the SS. (Schönherr, *Abenteuer*, 134)

The Protestant Church in the GDR opposed the anti-Israeli policy of the Communist government imposed by the Soviet Union, which interpreted the Jewish state as the spearhead of contemporary capitalism. After the vote at the United Nations equating Zionism with racism, the Protestant Church in the GDR — as we noted in chapter 1 — introduced the commemoration of the 9th of November in the local congregations. The spirit of Stuttgart and Darmstadt would not allow the Church to forget the German past, even though — as Schönherr repeatedly mentioned — not even the Darmstadt declaration had mentioned Auschwitz and the mass murder of the Jews. The Church in the GDR looked upon Israel as an island of safety for a people persecuted to death.

The Communist government honored the Jews living in the GDR for their antifascist background. The Jews who died in the death camps were named and remembered as antifascists, not as Jews. This may not have been an injustice in regard to Jews who had been active in the Communist Party and who were imprisoned, tortured, and killed because of their political commitment. But for ideological reasons, the government did not recognize motives for resisting fascism other than Communism. The victims of Hitler's terror who died simply because they were Jews — or those who died as Christian witnesses — were publicly listed as antifascists.

Heinrich Fink, a Protestant theologian with sympathy for the ruling party (SED) until 1985, strongly expressed his and the Church's disagreement with the anti-Israel policy of the government.[3] He offered theological reasons for his solidarity with Israel. He argued that the biblical message itself created a bond between the people of Israel and the Christian community. In the eyes of the East German ideologues, this theology made Fink a Zionist. Yet he and other leading church personalities were successful in persuading the government to expand the exhibitions built on the sites of the Nazi concentration camps at Buchenwald and Sachsenhausen, to include besides the war against Communism, the persecution of the Jews. The Church was the only community in the GDR that honored the Jews as bearers of a religious tradition and as witnesses reminding the nation of its dark and terrible past.

At the same time, the Church did not propose an exaggerated and therefore false concept of collective guilt. The personal culpability of Germans for Hitler's terror varied in accordance with their involvement in the fascist project. But even the Germans not directly involved, the Church argued, sinned by their silence and inaction. It was, after all, this massive passivity accompanied by bureaucratic obedience that made possible the rapid and efficient execution of Hitler's colossal crimes. Even courageous Germans who resisted and survived wondered, after the war, whether they had been courageous enough. While sin was indeed universal — the Church spoke of a *Mitschuld,* a participation in guilt — the Church refused to speak of Germany's collective guilt.

Speaking of collective guilt may prevent individuals from honestly confronting their own personal history. Such a discourse, moreover, would create confusion, since guilt cannot be attributed to people who were children during the war or who were born after the war. But has the new generation the right to shrug its shoulders in regard to the German past? Is there not a burden that all Germans, and in particular all Christian Germans, must bear?

The answer to these questions was offered in a statement of September 1979, made by the Protestant Church of both Germanies, introducing the concept of "a community of liability" (*Haftungsgemeinschaft*) (Schönherr, *Abenteuer,* 109). While children are not responsible

---

3. Bernhard Maleck, *Heinrich Fink* (Berlin: Dietz, 1992), 19-22.

for what their parents have done and hence bear no guilt, they are nonetheless bound to pay for the damage caused by their parents' misdeeds. They are morally held to pay the debt and offer restitution. The family is a community of liability: because of a strong sense of solidarity, families assume responsibility for the harm done by their ancestors and willingly make reparation. The greater the sense of solidarity, the more willingly the community accepts its liability. Nations are also communities of liability. Because of the spiritual bond of faith and baptism, churches are communities of liability in an even stronger sense. Here are the words of Bishop Schönherr addressing the congregation at Dresden in 1983, commemorating the destruction of their city:

> We are not a community of guilt. It would be unjust and unhistorical to attribute guilt and coresponsibility to the younger generation who did not live through those terrible years, except possibly as children. Yet we are a community of liability. We cannot appear before the world as members of the German people without the others saying to themselves: these are Germans, we know their history! Whether we like it or not — they will remember our terrible history for years to come. They will be afraid of us. We carry our history in our bodies — our beautiful, rich, and great history — Weimar, Wittenberg, Nürnberg, and Aachen. But we equally bear with us our dark and horrifying recent history of Coventry and Stalingrad, Buchenwald and Auschwitz. (Schönherr, *Abenteuer*, 128)

It is not easy to translate the German word *Vergangenheitsbewältigung*. It means confronting one's past and acknowledging one's guilt, and in doing so, being set free to move forward in a new spirit. This is the wrestling that vast numbers of Germans engaged in after the war. The Church regarded this wrestling with the past as part of its spiritual life of faith: without it, God's grace would not be available. Nor would there be a new beginning. The Kirchenbund used many opportunities to reflect on Germany's past and to draw the appropriate conclusions.

One such occasion was the 50th anniversary of the Barmen Declaration made by the Confessing Church in 1934. In 1984 the Protestant Church of both Germanies made a joint statement remembering the horror of the past, the faith of Barmen, and its meaning for the contemporary situation.[4] More startling were the public meetings in May 1985, in which the Kirchenbund commemorated the 40th anniversary of the end of the war. Here the accent was on wrestling with the past to render possible reconciliation and the restoration of friendship. Forgiving your enemies and seeking friendship with those from whom you have been estranged is a condition for reconciliation with God. Since the Germans had suffered under the brutality of the Soviet soldiers, and more importantly, since millions of Germans had been chased from lands in Central and Eastern Europe where their ancestors had settled several centuries ago, reconciliation with the Russians demanded of Germans the willingness to return to their political past and again recognize the massive crimes of Nazi aggression.

Bishop Johannes Hempel, preaching on May 8, 1985, in Berlin's Marienkirche, took up this painful topic. We are helped in this process, he said, by recalling personal experiences of reconciliation. On May 8, 1945, he himself, a 16-year-old soldier, woke up in a ditch near a small Czech town and saw for the first time in his life a Russian soldier sitting next to him. He was afraid. The Russian, eating his bread, did not smile. After a few moments, he turned and gave the young German a piece of his bread, adding in Russian, "Fellow, go home." Bishop Hempel mentioned other, more public moments of grace: the visit in Dresden soon after the war of English Christians who wanted to help clean up the rubble; the arrival of ecumenical leaders from former enemy countries to meet German churchmen in search of reconciliation; and the Stuttgart Declaration, composed in response to their initiative. In the spirit of Stuttgart and Darmstadt, the Kirchenbund had sought and found reconciliation with the churches in the Soviet Union and the countries of Eastern Europe. "Let us be reconciled with God and be grateful for the first steps that have been taken. We pray for strength to move forward in the future" (*Gemeinsam*, 203-207).

On May 10, 1985, Bishop Albrecht Schönherr spoke at the monument on Berlin's Grosse Hamburger Strasse where a Jewish old peoples' home stood at one time, the place where later the Nazis assembled the

---

4. *Gemeinsam unterwegs. Dokumente aus der Arbeit des BEK in der DDR* (Berlin: Evangelische Verlagsanstalt, 1989), 201. Subsequent references to this work will be made parenthetically in the text.

Jewish citizens before transporting them to the death camps. In a moving speech he imagined himself a Jew among the others and described what it was like to be humiliated, pushed into a train; to arrive at Auschwitz, be separated from your family, and enter into pain, darkness, and death. "I am deeply shaken," Schönherr continued. "This was done to these fellow human beings, and I did not oppose it." He claimed that he had no alibi, even if he was a member of the Confessing Church and tried to help his Jewish friends. He did not protest when in April 1933 the SA stood in front of Jewish stores; he did not cry out when in November 1938 the SA set fire to the synagogues and vandalized Jewish businesses; he did not inquire during the war where in the East the deported were being taken. What he hears today, and every time he thinks of these events, is God's question: Where is your bother Abel? "Our people bear on the forehead the mark of Cain for the factory-efficient murder of millions of Jews." It is, therefore, far too early to speak of reconciliation. We cannot be forgiven yet; we are only at the beginning; we still have to remove many obstacles. Let no one say, I have nothing to do with this any more. Unless we remember, drop our hypocrisy, and move forward toward the truth, we will not be reconciled with God (*Gemeinsam*, 207-208).

On the same day, May 10, 1985, Bishop Gottfried Forck gave an address at the concentration camp of Sachsenhausen, in which he offered a similar analysis of the absence of German resistance against the cruelty and crimes of Hitler's National-Socialists. Germans must never forget, the Church must never forget, for without remembrance and repentance there will be no reconciliation with God and no divine grace to persevere in the way of peace (*Gemeinsam*, 211-214).

A more difficult task was performed by Bishop Christof Stier, speaking on the same day at the cemetery in Halle where more than 20,000 German soldiers and civilians, killed in a fierce battle in 1945, were buried in nameless graves. After the war, Stier remembered, it was almost impossible to speak of our own sorrow; for then we were just finding out the endless suffering we Germans had inflicted upon other people. We were then silent because we were ashamed, or possibly because we thought it politically unwise. We never mourned our dead in freedom, and this repression often produces melancholy. Today, Stier continued, a Christian assembly commemorates in Berlin the mass murder of the Jews, and another one remembers the victims of concentration camps at Sachsenhausen. In this context, we freely mourn our own dead. We seek to be reconciled with our past, knowing that this means opposing war and standing for peace (*Gemeinsam*, 211-213). Like all bishops and theologians representing the Kirchenbund, Christof Stier recognized that faith and inwardness have a political dimension. He understood even mourning the dead killed during the war as a spiritual preparation for mutual understanding, justice, and peace.

On the same day, May 10, 1985, Bishop Christoph Demke spoke at the enormous cemetery on the heights of Seelow where the fallen soldiers of the Red Army were buried. Here another group of Christians were being asked to wrestle with their past, to repent, and to forgive; for only as they did this would they find their way toward God's future. "It is not easy to acknowledge that in our own midst, a land with so many churches, contempt for human beings brought forth a regime that dared to treat humans as cattle, hunt them as deer, and drive them from hearth and home to create a wider living space (*Lebensraum*) according to its own ideological and economic plans" (*Gemeinsam*, 215). With the Kirchenbund, Christoph Demke followed the spirit of Stuttgart and Darmstadt. This was the perspective from which he and the other churchmen read the Bible, looked upon historical events, and formulated the Christian message.

CHAPTER 5

The Humanistic Ideals of Socialism

That the Protestant Church in the GDR called itself "a church in socialism" (*Kirche im Sozialismus*) was well known in the world-wide ecumenical movement. This expression gave rise to the illusion in my mind that Protestant theology in the GDR actually resembled Latin American liberation theology. What I had to learn was that "socialism" in the GDR had a very specific meaning: it referred to the official Marxism-Leninism of the SED, the ruling Communist party. Socialism was equated with the theoretical positions and political decisions taken year after year by the central committee of the SED. There was no room whatever for alternative interpretations of socialism. These were denounced as heresies. The SED condemned both Tito's view that each country had its own way of entering into socialism and the views of Western socialists, who wanted to integrate Western democratic practices and controlled market mechanisms into the socialist society of the future. Following the Soviet model, the SED left no room for ideological pluralism. While in the West many Christians called themselves socialist according to a variety of definitions, in the GDR only Christians identified with the official Marxism-Leninism, such as members of the Pfarrerbund mentioned above, called themselves socialist. These Christians constituted a small minority. The Kirchenbund and the theology associated with it never called itself socialist.

*   *   *

Where did the expression, "a church in socialism," come from, and what did it mean? This question was asked in the GDR by young Christians in the early eighties who were not acquainted with the history of the Kirchenbund. To reply to them, the Study Commission of the Kirchenbund, with Ruth Zander as principal author, prepared an informative 40-page document, made available in mimeographed form, on the history of the term *Kirche im Sozialismus* as used by the Bund, by theologians, and by representatives of the government.

In chapter 3 we saw that for pastoral reasons in the late fifties the Protestant Church wrestled with the discernment of place (*Ortsbestimmung*). The joint communiqué published by church and state in 1958 already contained a paragraph saying that the Protestant churches approved the peace initiatives of the GDR and "respected the development toward socialism."[1] In 1960 Walter Ulbricht, then the state president, made a public statement on the relation between church and state with the title, "No contradiction between Christianity and the humanistic aims of socialism," in which he urged the churches in the GDR to distance themselves from West Germany as it assumed an ever greater place in NATO's military plans.[2] Ulbricht desired greater support from the Church for his policy of delimitation (*Abgrenzung*). As mentioned in chapter 1, Ulbricht had a conversation with the Protestant theologian Emil Fuchs, who was favorably disposed toward the government and who at that occasion delivered a letter to Ulbricht signed by thousands of church workers, clergy and laity, expressing agreement with the government's proposal for common social and humanistic responsibility and recommending greater cooperation between Christians and Marxists.[3] Emil Fuchs here represented a position close to that of the Pfarrerbund. Ulbricht's second conversation was with Bishop Mitzenheim, who did not share the Pfarrerbund's commitment to socialism, but who, as an orthodox Lutheran, obedient to Romans 13, had great respect for the state, including the socialist one.

1. Reinhard Henkys, *Bund der evangelischen Kirchen in der DDR. Dokumente zu seiner Entstehung* (Berlin: Eckart Verlag, 1970), 50.

2. Henkys, 51.

3. Robert F. Goeckel, *The Lutheran Church and the East-German State* (Ithaca, NY: Cornell University Press, 1990), 60.

When, toward the end of the sixties, the government proposed a new constitution, one more in line with its Communist orientation, the churches were afraid they would lose the recognition as public institutions granted by the old constitution of 1949. Just before the bishops met at Kloster Lehnin in February 1968 to draft their response to the government's proposal, Bishop Mitzenheim made his own public statement: "We do not want to be a church *against* socialism, but rather a church *for* the citizens of the GDR who wish to live as Christians in a socialist society with an unoffended conscience."[4] The bishops' Letter of Lehnin addressed to the state president contained the following sentences:

> As citizens of the GDR and as Christians we accept as starting point for all reflection that after the War started through German guilt there now exist two German states. . . . As citizens of the socialist state, we are challenged by the task to make socialism a more just form of human interaction (*eine Gestalt gerechteren Zusammenlebens*). (Zander, 2)

The Communist government, supported by the CDU (East), interpreted these statements as a new openness of the Church to the policies of the SED. Commenting early in 1969 on the massive support given by the population to the new socialist constitution, Hans Seigewasser, state secretary for church questions, made a public statement saying that church leaders "ought to conclude from this that the spiritual mission of the church in socialism (*Kirche im Sozialismus*) demands that they not repudiate socialism, its humanistic policies, or its international relations" (Zander, 2). This was the first time that the term *Kirche im Sozialismus* had been used. Gerald Götting, leader of the CDU (East), repeated the hope that the church leaders would learn their lesson from the popular support for socialism. Knowing that the churches had decided to create their own federation, Seigewasser and Götting wanted to influence the orientation of the new ecclesiastical body.

4. Ruth Zander, "Zum Gebrauch des Begriffes Kirche im Sozialismus" (Berlin: Bund der Evangelischen Kirchen, 1988), 2. Subsequent references to this work will be given parenthetically in the text.

Socialism was not mentioned in the *Ordnung* (founding document) of the Kirchenbund or at its first Synod in the fall of 1969. But because of the discourse adopted by the CDU (East) and the Pfarrerbund, and because the government's idea that the Church had chosen a new orientation, the Kirchenbund had to clarify its relationship to socialism. A church assembly in 1970 stated that "the Bund had to prove itself as a community of witness and service in the socialist society of the GDR," and in the report of the Synod of 1971 we read, "A community of witness and service made up of churches in the GDR must carefully discern its location: *in* this society thus shaped, *not beside* it, *not against* it. This church community must preserve the freedom of its witness and service" (Zander, 4; italics added).

These phrases, despite their brevity, reveal the Bund's preoccupation with pastoral concerns. Several attitudes still found among East German Christians are here excluded. One such attitude existed among certain church members who refused to accept the division of Germany, favored a strong anti-Communist discourse, and longed for an early collapse of the GDR. Their attitude, the Bund held, was not based on an appropriate discernment of place. The Bund disapproved of the total rejection of the socialist society: it did not intend to define itself as the opposition in the GDR. Secondly, the Bund excluded the attitude of Christians who wanted the Church to withdraw from society and restrict its pastoral ministry to the protection and promotion of the shrinking community of believers. Thirdly, speaking of the Church *in* rather than *for* socialism, the Bund excluded the uncritical surrender to SED ideology and policy found in the CDU (East) and the Pfarrerbund. The Bund refused to conform to the government's official theory and practice, not only because of its materialistic philosophy, but also because the Bund resisted on principle full integration into the political system, any political system. This, as we shall see, was in keeping with the Barmen Declaration of 1934.

What this triple exclusion — not against, not beside, not for — meant in practical terms was that the Bund wanted to obtain a free social space in the GDR, a space defined by the freedom and the bondage of the gospel, from which the Christian community could address society, support public policies that merited Christian approval, and criticize public policies that offended the Christian conscience.

Displeased with this development — and for other reasons mentioned in chapter 1 — the socialist state waited until 1971 before it acknowledged the Kirchenbund. When this recognition did take place, Paul Verner, secretary of the SED's Central Committee, articulated the government's approach to church questions. Approving the churches' decision to create their own federation in the GDR, the government reminded them of the following five points, (1) that when the churches discuss their relation to socialism, this must refer to the concretely existing socialist society of the GDR, (2) that a negotiated understanding between the state and the church does not imply an abandonment of the philosophical vision on either side, (3) that the Church may not locate itself in a neutral position between capitalism and socialism, but must exercise its ministry in keeping with the constitution and social aims of the GDR, (4) that the more positive and unambiguous the Church's relation to socialism becomes, the less it will be contradicted by its members who see themselves as socialist, and (5) that a church that supports the humanistic aims and peace initiatives of the GDR is likely to gain the confidence of its government. Most interesting in Paul Verner's speech was the following sentence: "While there has existed in the past a Prussification of the Protestant churches and a nationalistic — yes, even a fascist falsification of the Christian message — a 'socialization' has as yet never existed, nor will it ever exist in the future" (Zander, 5).

The Synod of 1973 replied to Verner's remarks:

> We are citizens of a socialist state and members of a socialist society. . . . We want to be "a church, not *beside* nor *against,* but *in* socialism." This formula has been approved by our partner, the state, and made more precise by adding that "a 'socialization' of the Christian message has as yet never existed, nor will it ever exist in the future." This would mean that there is no room for "a socialist church" or "a socialist theology." It would therefore be pointless to expect the churches or individual Christians to bless with pious phrases . . . political measures taken without consulting them. Church within socialism is the church that helps Christians and their congregations to find their way in the socialist society in the freedom and bondage of their faith and to do their best for all and for society as a whole. *Kirche im Sozialismus* is the church that is ready in the

freedom of faith to cooperate gladly with efforts to improve human life and, where necessary, to ward off dangers to human life in our society. Yet as experience has shown, Christians looking at the world in the light of God's promises and under God's command may see problems or hear questions differently from those who perceive and evaluate the world from a different perspective. (Zander, 6)

The government, committed to its own socialist orthodoxy, always refused to dialogue with religious philosophies and alternative socialist theories. While it favored cooperation between Marxists and Christians in the GDR, it refused to accept the invitations to dialogue on philosophical issues addressed to it by the Church. For this reason, the government looked with great suspicion upon the various forms of political and liberationist theology of the West.[5] In 1976 a visit by Dorothee Sölle in Berlin (East) created difficulties for the Church. In an article written after 1989, the author, who had been formerly employed as an official censor, explains that while conservative Christian literature could be imported without difficulty, the critical theology of Johann-Baptist Metz, Jürgen Moltmann, Dorothee Sölle, and others was strictly prohibited.[6]

*   *   *

The Kirchenbund opted for what was sometimes called the narrow ridge between total assimilation and total repudiation. In reality this ridge was not so narrow: it allowed for a spectrum of choices, some of which put greater stress on the common humanistic aims and on cooperation between Christians and Maxists; while others emphasized more the critical perspective, articulating the extent to which the existing socialism did not live up to its own ideals and principles.

Let us compare how two Protestant leaders and good friends, Bishop Albrecht Schönherr and Provost Heino Falcke, interpreted the bold path between total assimilation and total rejection. While both

5. Goeckel, 196.
6. See P. Kokschal, "Veröffentlichungen unter staatlicher Zensur," in *Unter kommunistischer Zensur,* Theologisches Jahrbuch 1991, ed. W. Ernst et al. (Leipzig: Benno Verlag, 1992), 16-22.

were faithful representatives of the Bund's theology, they were evaluated by the Communist government in different ways. The government preferred Schönherr. When he became bishop of Berlin-Brandenburg, leaving Bishop Kurt Scharf in charge of West Berlin, the government was pleased. As the Kirchenbund's first president, remaining in office till 1981, Schönherr was the principal spokesman for the Church, addressed the government at many occasions, and acted as principal negotiator with state president Erich Honecker on March 6, 1978. Schönherr wanted a free social space for the Church. He emphasized discerning cooperation with Marxists from case to case; he also offered a critique of SED socialism and denounced the continuing discrimination suffered by Christians in clear, but diplomatic language. Because he convinced the government that the Church need not be a hostile force in the GDR, the government looked upon him with a certain favor.

By contrast, Heino Falcke was regarded as a troublesome critic by the government. Falcke was a theologian, a teacher involved in clergy education, and the president of the Commission on Church and Society set up by the Bund. That Falcke annoyed the government was dramatically revealed by its swift reaction to an address given at the Synod at Dresden in 1972, in which he spoke of the Christian hope for "an improvable socialism." When the government forbade the publication of the text, the Bund decided — to avoid repression and retain its freedom — not to print it in the Synod's proceedings, but only to hand it out to the participants in mimeographed form. The government looked upon Falcke with a certain disfavor.

When we read the published speeches and papers of Schönherr and Falcke, we find that the two churchmen are in basic agreement: they both walk the path between total surrender and total opposition. They express in very similar terms their identification with the humanistic ideals of socialism and their theological critique of the existing socialist system. Still, taking a closer look at how these two Christian thinkers presented the socialist challenge reveals that the chosen path of the Kirchenbund made room for several options.

Bishop Schönherr expressed his views on the Church's approach to the socialist society in several speeches, including the addresses given at meetings where the executive committee of the Bund was received by the Communist government.[7] I shall divide his views into several categories: (1) the unbridgeable gulf between Christian faith and socialist theory; (2) the need for Christian-Marxist cooperation in the GDR; (3) the ethical imperative implicit in Christian-Marxist dialogue; (4) the things Christians learn from this dialogue; and (5) the reformable character of GDR socialism.

1. The first point that strikes the reader is the Bishop's emphasis on the unbridgeable gulf between the two worldviews, Christian faith and Marxism-Leninism. He acknowledged that it was a great burden for Christians to live in a society defined by an atheist philosophy and to participate in institutions such as the school system that expressed and communicated this atheism. At the same time, Schönherr was glad that the government itself acknowledged the unbridgeable gulf and hence made no attempt to integrate the Church into the social system. For Schönherr, a member of the Confessing Church during the Nazi period, the Communist government's global rejection of Christianity was by far preferable to Hitler's attempt, with his constant reference to "the Almighty" and "divine Providence," to woo the churches and to integrate them into his fascist political project. Schönherr was pleased that the Communist government recognized that the Christian church could never be socialist. The Church, as we saw, defined itself *in* socialism, not *against* it, nor *beside* it, nor *for* it. What the Church needed was a free space in Communist society.

Schönherr was critical of the CDU (East) and a small minority of Christians who overlooked or disguised the radical difference between Christianity and Marxism-Leninism. He consequently rejected their proposal that Christians in the GDR should call themselves "socialist citizens of Christian faith" (Schönherr, *Abenteuer,* 318).

2. Schönherr believed in the cooperation of Christians with their secular cocitizens, Marxists though they be, in the building of a more

7. Schönherr addressed the minister for church questions in 1971 when the government finally acknowledged the Kirchenbund (Schönherr, *Horizont und Mitte. Aufsätze, Vorträge, Reden, 1953-1977* [München: Chr. Kaiser Verlag, 1979], 250-259, see also 260-269) and the state president, Erich Honecker, at the negotiation of the March 6, 1978 (Schönherr, *Abenteuer der Nachfolge. Reden und Aufsätze, 1978-1988* [Berlin: Wichern-Verlag, 1988], 272-277, see also 277-290; subsequent references to this work are given parenthetically in the text).

just and humane society. The Bund's self-understanding as a community of witness and service demanded that Christians be present in society, giving witness to God's coming reign and standing in solidarity with the marginal and disenfranchised. Since according to God's providence the Church's location was in the GDR, and since there were no empty spaces on God's geographic map, it was in the socialist society that the Church had to exercise its ministry. Schönherr developed the notion of the Church's "presence" in the GDR; that is to say, the Church's participation in the successes and difficulties, hopes and fears, achievements and failures of the state and its citizens (Schönherr, *Abenteuer*, 324.) Even if Christians were now a minority, they included the whole of society in their concern and recognized their coresponsibility for its future development.

But if the Church rejects the materialist vision of Communist society, how can it urge its members to cooperate with Marxists? There was a good reason why Schönherr regarded this as a crucial question. He severely judged Christians during the Nazi period, among them members of the Confessing Church, who rejected the idolatrous dimension of German fascism and Hitler's attempt to control the Church, yet who still cooperated in a selective way in the building of fascist Germany. For Schönherr, the crucial difference between these two historical situations was that fascism offered a vision of domination and exclusion; while socialism was born of a dream of cooperation and equality. In their Letter from Lehnin, the bishops had acknowledged their respect for socialism as "a more just form of human interaction."

Schönherr was impressed by the biblical roots of the socialist vision: a society beyond man's exploitation of man, a society of justice and equality, a society of collective responsibility, assuring the material well-being and the humanistic development of all its members. He was confirmed in this position by the theology of the WCC which — as we shall see — interpreted the biblical promise of "shalom" as God's coming reign, pacifying and reconciling the whole of humanity.

Still, Schönherr anguished about the call to cooperation with Marxists. He wondered why most churchmen in the West did not anguish over cooperation with capitalists, and he was puzzled by the ease with which Christians in the West endorsed the liberal dream of freedom and competition. After much soul searching, Schönherr concluded that the Church in the GDR should not stress its opposition to atheist materialism, but instead give priority to witness and service in the name of Christ. While Christians remained critical of the system, they were called to cooperate. Here is a sentence written by Schönherr and repeated by him at subsequent occasions: "If the aim is a more just, more peaceful, and more friendly world, and if we know that cooperating in this is God's will, then we need not take the limits of the ideology more seriously than the common task."[8] Cooperation, therefore, does not imply forgetting the problematic nature of the materialist project. Cooperation is never to be offered out of a total endorsement of the system. It must always retain its conditional character. Schönherr writes:

> The church in socialism wants to help its Christian members to find their way in this society. It wants to reflect with them in concrete terms how this way can be found "in the freedom and the bondage of faith." . . . As church in socialism, it wants to support everything in this society that fosters human life, and warn it of all that could threaten human life. The Church affirms its right to utter a frank Yes, and given the case, an equally frank No. Heino Falcke . . . has called this "critical solidarity" and Werner Krusche "discriminating cooperation." (Schönherr, *Abenteuer*, 324)

Schönherr held that the notion of the church as "watchman" over society, sometimes used in the past and occasionally proposed by members of the Bund, was not appropriate. Following the spirit of Stuttgart and Darmstadt, the Bishop disagreed with the claim that the church saw more clearly than the world the dangers and destructive possibilities of the future. The church, he argued, must not present itself as a teacher who knows everything better. Christians must admit that they participate in the errors and confusion of the world.

3. Schönherr favored dialogue with Marxists. He regretted that the government, while willing to negotiate with the Church, refused to engage in dialogue on fundamental issues. Still, in a nonofficial way, dialogue between Christians and Marxists did take place. Schönherr believed that implicit in dialogue were certain ethical imperatives. This

---

8. Schönherr, *Horizont und Mitte*, 269; *Abenteuer*, 273.

was true for ecumenical dialogue among Christians as well as for Christian-Marxist dialogue. True conversation demands that we take our partners seriously, assume their good faith unless we have evidence to the contrary, and interpret what they say from their point of view. Dialogue demands respect for the other.

Schönherr recognized that this was not easy for Christians who had been taught to fear Communism and had studied it only in order to refute it. Since Communist regimes had persecuted Christians, there was good reason to be afraid of them. But did this hostility, Schönherr asked, describe the total reality of Communism in the GDR? This would have to be investigated. Dialogue, he held, was the only way to uncover the historical reality of socialism in East Germany. Schönherr believed that Christians were empowered by the Holy Spirit to overcome their fear and enter with confidence into this conversation.

The divine promise to liberate the oppressed and disenfranchised, he argued, was realized in a twofold action, the outer liberation from unjust structures and, often prior to that, the inner liberation of the marginalized, the gift of the Spirit that allowed them to shake off their fears and false perceptions of themselves and affirm themselves in freedom. The Church in the socialist society of the GDR was thus freed by the Spirit to enter into dialogue with the official Marxism-Leninism.

Implicit in dialogue is the recognition that just as you learn much through the ongoing conversation, so does your partner. Christians have a tendency to think that Communists never change. Schönherr wondered if Christians who defended this position most ardently were themselves incapable of changing. If Christians overcame their suspicion that all Communists said and did was nothing but propaganda, dialogue would lead them to important discoveries.

As an example, the Bishop discussed the decision of the government in the late seventies to honor Germany's cultural past by rebuilding some of the famous churches destroyed in the war and, more surprisingly, by commemorating the quincentenary of Luther's birth in 1983. The immediate reaction of many Christians, especially in the West, was to interpret this new interest as state propaganda. Schönherr assumed good faith on the part of the Communist government. Basing

himself on a report of Christoph Demke written for the Kirchenbund,[9] Schönherr explained why Marxists tried to relate socialism to
the cultural heritage of humanity. According to the Constitution of
the GDR, "the socialist society fosters the cultural life of the working
population, cultivates the humanistic values of the national cultural
heritage and the world culture, and fosters the cultural development
as a benefit for the whole people." The SED convention of 1976 made
this statement: "The socialist culture of the GDR is indebted to the
rich heritage produced throughout the entire history of the German
people. Whatever is great and noble, humanistic and revolutionary is
honored and brought forward in the GDR by setting it in living
relation to the tasks of the present" (Schönherr, *Abenteuer,* 279).

Going more deeply into Marxist-Leninist theory, Schönherr explained the meaning of three terms, "inheritance," "tradition" and
"mediation." Inheritance refers to creative events and monuments of
the past in which humanity has revealed its greatness and high ideals.
Tradition refers to a selection and a particular reading of the inheritance,
in accordance with the interests of a class or a community. While great
deeds, art, and religion have usually been interpreted by powerful elites
or ruling classes and used to bolster their power, they were also read,
though quite differently, by traditions linked to popular groups and
people in resistance. Even Christian history reveals the presence of
radical traditions. In the Communist literature of GDR, Schönherr
recalled, Thomas Münzer and the radical wing of the Reformation have
long been appreciated, while Luther was seen largely as a defender of
the feudal order.

Can the rich heritage of great deeds, art, and religion be revived?
Since the only access to the past is contextual, the recovery of the
inheritance takes place through "mediation." Mediation here refers to
a reading of these great events that uncovers values capable of inspiring
and guiding people in the present to deal creatively with the problems
of their society. Can this search for mediation, Schönherr asked, be
simply denigrated as propaganda? Is this not how every national and
religious community relates itself to its own past? A new reading of

---

9. *Gemeinsam unterwegs. Dokumente aus der Arbeit des BEK in der DDR* (Berlin:
Evangelische Verlagsanstalt, 1989), 192-200.

Luther, Schönherr argued, has allowed German Communists to appreciate his greatness. Despite his political blindness, they now see in Luther a major cultural innovator who liberated the people from foreign ecclesiastical control and who created a new ethos of duty and hard work in the service of society. Such a secular reading of Luther makes theologians a little uncomfortable, Schönherr added, but at least it explains to them why Communists, on their part, feel a little uncomfortable when Christians use certain classical texts of Marx in support of their theology.

4. In dialogue with Marxists, Christians have much to learn. In chapter 3 we saw that Schönherr had definite ideas of what such learning meant for Christian preaching and teaching. He also used his discussion of the new Communist approach to Luther to show how fruitful dialogue can be for the Christian partner. What he himself had learned was the changing evaluation of religion in recent Marxist literature. In the past, Marxist-Leninists looked upon religion as false consciousness produced in people by the misery and self-alienation inflicted on them by exploitative structures: religion was opium. Yet in the seventies, Marxist literature began to think of religion as rooted in deep human needs: the effort to cope with suffering, sickness, and death and the quest for a unified meaning of life in which to find strength and security (Schönherr, *Abenteuer*, 282). While these Marxist authors still believed that religion would eventually give way to a more scientific self-understanding, they did not expect this to happen soon. Since religion would remain alive in socialism for a long time, these authors recommended that the state acknowledge the churches as "partners" in its social project.

That religion is rooted in deep human needs is a position that raises difficult theological questions. All Christians believe that the gospel is God's free gift to humanity caught in sin, but they differ as to whether this free gift can be said to correspond to and fulfill humanity's deepest yearning. Lutheran and Barthian theologies have tended to stress the discontinuity between God's grace and human longing, between divine *agape* and human *eros,* between the obedience of faith and the search for human fulfillment. It is therefore surprising that in his reply to these Marxist thinkers, the Lutheran Bishop concedes — as a Catholic theologian would — that the Christian religion indeed corresponds to human longing. Schönherr offers a biblical argument for this. Jesus himself related his message to human desires: he offered himself as bread; as light; as thirst-quenching fountain; as way, truth, and life. Jesus promised to fulfill the great human longing, yet this fulfillment by far exceeded human expectation. That is why, the Bishop argued, the gospel need not be afraid of competition, even when it is preached in a society where people's material and cultural needs are largely fulfilled: for the gift of the Spirit by far transcends the human horizon.

5. Schönherr believed that the socialism of the GDR was reformable. He pointed to the changed situation of the Church in the GDR from the repression and uncertainty experienced in the fifties, through the creation and public recognition of the Kirchenbund in the late sixties and early seventies, to the agreement of March 6, 1978, and the Church's enjoyment of a relatively free social space in the subsequent years. Even Catholic churchmen in the GDR, more cautious than the Bund in regard to the socialist state, acknowledged that changes were taking place in the policies of the government.[10] The Polish pope himself, John Paul II, looking at the world in the eighties, believed that the two antithetical world systems, capitalist and socialist, were here to stay; and that both of them were reformable.[11] We know now that Schönherr, the pope, and the rest of the world made a mistake: they did not foresee that the Soviet Union and Soviet bloc socialism were about to collapse.

*   *   *

Heino Falcke's approach to the existing socialism agreed with Albrecht Schönherr's. Falcke insisted on the unbridgeable gulf between Christian faith and Marxist ideology; he recognized the need for the cooperation of Christians with Marxists; he supported the dialogue of Christians with Marxists with its implicit ethical imperative; he acknowledged that there was much Christians could learn from certain tenets of Marxism;

---

10. Joachim Wanke, "Glaubenserfahrung aus der Zeit des DDR-Sozialismus," *Lebendiges Zeugnis,* Schriftreihe der Akademischen Bonifatius-Einigung, Paderborn, 47 (May 1992): 60-61.

11. G. Baum and R. Ellsberg, eds., *The Logic of Solidarity* (Maryknoll, NY: Orbis Books, 1980).

and he believed that the existing socialism in the GDR was reformable. Where he differed somewhat from Schönherr — a difference that explains why he irritated the government — was in his more critical presentation of Christian-Marxist cooperation.

Let us turn first to Falcke's famous address at the 1972 Synod in Dresden.[12] In Schönherr's introduction to Falcke's *Mit Gott Schritt halten,* a collection of his speeches and papers, the Bishop wrote that this address now belongs to the theological foundation of the Kirchenbund (Falcke, 9). It developed theological arguments for an innovative understanding of the Church and its mission in the socialist society. We shall have occasion to return to these arguments further on. What interests us at the moment is Falcke's approach to socialism and his understanding of cooperation.

The starting point of Falcke's theology is that Christ liberates the church so that it can serve society — and destines the church to serve the liberation of humankind. The first obstacle of the church's mission lies within itself. The church still clings to the past, often to a sentimentalized version of it; the church still formulates the gospel in inherited terms without an effort to translate it into contemporary discourse; the church is still afraid of Marxism and refuses to take seriously the Marxist challenge; it is still worried about its collective identity so that it does not generate new, imaginative ways of living and cooperating with others. Yet though we are sinners, we are justified by faith in the Lord. Because we believe in Jesus Christ, liberator of his church, we rely on his promises and trust that we, the church, are reformable. Thanks to Christ's power, we are now willing to come to self-knowledge, even engage in dialogue with others and use social science to gain a better understanding of who we are collectively. Thanks to Christ's power, we are ready to leave the past behind, give up our former privileges, open ourselves to the discourse of our contemporaries, and proclaim the Good News in a manner that makes sense to them. Relying on Christ's power, we need not cautiously protect our own identity, but dare to forget ourselves in the love of others.

12. Heino Falcke, *Mit Gott Schritt halten: Reden und Aufsätze* (Berlin: Wichern-Verlag, 1986), 12-32. Subsequent references to this work will be made parenthetically in the text.

The service the church offers to the world is liberation, the liberation promised by Jesus Christ. Falcke argues that for the Protestant Church in the socialist society of GDR this means "mature cooperation" (*mündige Zusammenarbeit*). He recognizes that this is not what the government understands by cooperation. The government wants Christians to support its social vision and its practical policies, bringing from their religious background only motivation, but no ideas. Falcke finds this unacceptable. Christians may not sever their yearning for a more just society from their ideas of what such a society should be. Both socialism and liberalism, even if for different reasons, want to restrict the meaning of the Christian message to the private realm. Christians cannot agree with this. Falcke argues, therefore, that Christians may offer the socialist society cooperation only if they can do this from the perspective of the gospel, that is to say a mature, discriminating cooperation from case to case. The gospel protects Christians from uttering "a global Yes" or "a global No" to the existing socialism: it frees them from these paralysing alternatives. The gospel sends them on the daring path, in the freedom and bondage of faith, between total surrender and total repudiation.

Falcke echoes here the Reformed doctrine of Christ's kingship, even if he does not mention it specifically. Christians believe, he argues, that Christ is present in the world, even in the socialist society which ignores him. Christ's kingship is universal: his realm on earth is not confined to the church. But in what does his rule consist? According to Falcke, wherever a transition is taking place from unjust to more just social conditions, wherever people are freed from the burden of oppression and exploitation, Jesus Christ is at work ruling, or perhaps better serving, humanity.

Left to itself, this teaching could encourage a one-sided theology: Christians might come to think that Christ's rule exhausts itself in secular justice. That is why Falcke invokes the Lutheran doctrine of the two kingdoms (Falcke, 23), adding at once that the distinction between secular justice and divine salvation must not be understood as a total separation. When socialists propose that the just society they envisage liberates people not only from economic exploitation but also and at the same time from all human self-alienation, Christians protest that this claim is excessive, unbelievable, even idolatrous. Christians may listen to and learn from the socialist message, they may cooperate with socialists in creating conditions of greater justice, but they believe that the socialist message of secular salvation is bound to reveal itself as false and disappoint those who cling to it. There exists no this-worldly salvation, Falcke insists. Unless people recognize the fallibility of their ideas and the ambiguous character of their social engagement, unless they recognize their sinfulness and need for forgiveness, they are on the way toward their own destruction.

Falcke continues. Troubled by the fixity of the socialist ideology and yet relying on Christ's presence in their society, Christians engage in mature cooperation from case to case "in the hope of an improvable socialism" (Falcke, 24). This was the sentence the government judged heretical. But equally, if not more provocative, was the final section of Falcke's address where he offered a more detailed description of what is meant by cooperation from the perspective of the gospel.

First, Christians partial to the marginal and disenfranchised would stand up for the disadvantaged even in the GDR. In the eighties, Heino Falcke persuaded the Bund with this argument to stand up for the critical groups organized in the churches, even if the Bund did not agree with all of their positions.

Second, Christian cooperation meant bringing up for discussion topics that were officially regarded as taboo in the GDR. In the early seventies, environmental devastation was still such a topic. In demanding room for an open public debate, Falcke, as well as Schönherr, always distinguished their own position from the political pluralism of Western society. There people were free to offer their personal ideas without necessarily being committed to the collective project of their society. Falcke called this the pluralism of inconsequentiality (*Belanglosigkeit*): the utterance of personal preferences without attachment to the common good. What Christians asked for in the GDR was different: they wanted a free discussion of ideas and policies among people committed in various ways to the socialist project.

Third, Christian cooperation demanded greater public availability of information. The government in control of the communication media limited information about what was happening in the GDR and the world in general, following a narrow understanding of its official ideology. Falcke argued that cooperation could not be intelligent unless it was based on exact information. The government slogan inviting people to "cooperate, coplan and corule" was utterly meaningless unless people had access to adequate information and room for a public debate.

Fourth, Christian cooperation raised the critical question of the work ethic in the GDR. Marxism wanted to deliver workers from the alienation of labor: workers were to become the subject of their labor; that is, participate in the decisions regarding their work and assume responsibility for the use of their products. But in the GDR, Falcke argued, workers were still ruled by "the achievement principle." While in capitalism workers had to achieve in accordance with decisions made by the owners of capital, in socialism — despite its promise — workers were not their own self-defining subjects, but had to achieve in accordance with the government's economic plan. Hence many of the social problems in the GDR, Falcke argued, were caused by the continuing alienation of labor and thus resembled the social malaise in Western societies.

Equally disturbing to the government, though fully in line with Schönherr's theology, was Falcke's paper written for the Kirchenbund in 1976 entitled, "Christian Faith and the Ideology of the Really Existing Socialism" (Falcke, 33-56). Here he offered extended critical reflections on socialist ideology and on what Christian cooperation should mean in the GDR.

Marxist ideology was for Christians unacceptable, even though there were themes in this ideology that had an affinity with Christian aspirations. Taking people's material conditions seriously and seeking to overcome economic poverty and exploitation were fully in keeping with the biblical message. So were solidarity with the oppressed in their struggle for emancipation, and the anticipation of a world transformed according to justice and peace. Falcke added that the word "transformation" had special meaning for Christians, for it recalled Christ's death and resurrection and suggested the believer's passage from sin to new life.

Because Christians believe in God's good creation, inherited sin, and Christ's saving work to redeem human history, their perspective has a certain affinity with the socialist vision of a reconciled, emancipated humanity. There is no equivalent Christian affinity with the capitalist vision of universal competition and the social evolution through the victory of the successful.

We note in passing that Falcke defended the nearness of Christians to the socialist vision on biblical grounds, invoking the theology of the divine shalom — to which we shall return later. Falcke specifically excluded the attempt of certain Protestant theologians, such as Emil Brunner, to rehabilitate the concept of natural law and to argue for social justice in terms of universal principles. For Falcke (and Schönherr) theology is always contextual: Christ is not a universal principle to be applied to concrete situations by people using their intelligence, but a living person, God's own Word, who addresses Christians in their historical context and summons forth the conversion of mind and heart, teaching them how to react and what to do.

Yet despite the affinity, Falcke always returns to the unbridgeable gap between Christian faith and Marxist ideology. For Marxists the movement toward emancipation follows a law built into history: human liberation is the outcome of necessity, not an ethical achievement based on divinely-supported human freedom. For Christians, by contrast, history remains forever open, open to human sin and the unpredictable way of grace.

Unacceptable for Christians are, secondly, the tenet that the proletariate is the so-called universal class initiating through its struggle the emancipation of humankind, and the tenet that the Communist Party is the only authentic interpreter of the proletariate's material interests. Christians find this unacceptable because they regard as excessive and ultimately idolatrous all universalist claims made by human groups and human institutions. (In passing, this is why Protestants even shudder at the infallibility of the Pope and the Catholic Church's claim, vigorously defended in the past, that it was the only medium of salvation.) According to Falcke, Christians also find the Marxist claims for the role of the proletariate unacceptable because it is not verified by the experience of the socialist countries where new structures of exclusion have replaced the old ones. He does not accept the Marxist explanation that the passage into freedom and the withering of the state must be preceded by an historical interlude, the dictatorship of the proletariate, the role of which is to prepare its own disappearance. Falcke argues that nothing in the experience of the socialist countries suggests that the state is reducing its role and preparing its eventual demise.

Unacceptable for Christians is, thirdly, the Marxist theory that the victory of the proletariate will lift humanity into the realm of freedom and initiate the overcoming of all alienation. Christians hold that because of the presence of sin in human life, the total deliverance of human self-alienation is not possible within history. Besides, people's rescue from self-estrangement, however partial, is not a purely secular process: it is related to Christ's redemptive work.

If the gulf between Christian faith and Marxist ideology is so wide, why then should Christians cooperate in the building of a more just GDR? Falcke offers two new arguments.

1. It is important to distinguish between Marxism-Leninism as ideology and as concrete social reality. Since the social reality is made up of a multitude of actions and decisions not directly derived from the ideology, the two never perfectly overlap; they remain related to one another and exist in a certain tension.[13] Falcke argues that Christians may not look at Marxism-Leninism simply as an ideology and forget that it is at the same time a social reality in history. Why not? First, because in the concrete society God continues to be at work and many good things do happen. Second, because it is possible to criticize the social reality and propose improvements without necessarily attacking the public ideology to which the government is committed. Christians must make use of such practical possibilities. Third, if Christians focus on the unacceptable ideology and refuse to attend to the concrete social conditions, they are apt to construct a counter-ideology, such as anti-Communism, liberalism, or Christian socialism, which would eventually lead to an ideologizing of the Christian faith. Christian faith, following the Barmen Declaration, can never be neatly fitted into any socio-political theory. What follows from these arguments is that Christians in the GDR, while recognizing the unbridgeable gulf, must attend to the concrete social conditions and cooperate with others in making this society more just, more humane, more capable of fulfilling people's rightful expectations.

13. The identical point is also made by Pope John Paul II in his encyclical of 1987, *Sollicitudo Socialis*. See Baum and Ellsberg, 115-116.

2. Falcke also takes a closer look at the notion of ideology. He introduces a distinction taken from the report of the "Church and Society" meeting held in 1968 at the WCC, at which the churches of the Third World were for the first time vocal participants. The first definition of ideology — which we applied above to Marxism-Leninism — is a set of ideas and values expressing the aspirations of a *particular* group that is given *universal* significance by using it to interpret the whole of human history. Ideologies absolutize a partial truth, and in this sense they misrepresent reality. Ideologies are surrogate religions. Christians look upon them as forms of idolatry.

Yet another way of looking at ideologies reveals that they are necessary instruments in any collective effort to transform the social order. Ideologies are hereby defined as sets of ideas and values, interpreting society and stimulating action, which remain open to new experiences and subsequent revisions. These ideologies lay no claim to finality. They do not pretend to interpret the whole of history. But they are indispensable instruments for organizing people in a joint struggle for social change: they reveal the ideal and direction of the common effort and summon forth commitment and loyalty. Ideologies thus defined make no ultimate statement on the human condition; they do not act as surrogate religions; they belong entirely to the realm of the penultimate.

Christians have no objections in principle to ideologies of the second kind.[14] In fact, every community engaged in a social project and every movement seeking social change has some sort of ideology promoting its unity and purpose, which normally does not make absolute claims. Of course, every ideology of this kind may be tempted to become a substitute religion. People must always act critically in their social location so that the ideology of their community does not become an idol, eventually demanding human sacrifices. Falcke argues that Christians in the GDR, by critically cooperating within the social reality, may — with the help of other citizens — transform the totalizing ideology of the government into an ideology of the second type, open to experience, debate, and revision.

14. The final report of the 1979 Latin American Bishops Conference at Puebla introduced the same distinction and arrived at the same conclusion. See J. Eagleson and P. Scharper, eds., *Puebla and Beyond* (Maryknoll, NY: Orbis Books, 1979), 198.

Falcke regards cooperation as a Christian duty in the GDR. From the preceding, it is already clear that what he has in mind is a special kind of cooperation. He called it "mature cooperation," rejecting "a global Yes" and "a global No," critical from case to case. He specifically rejects a cooperation he chooses to call "partial identification." By this he refers to the strategy of assimilation adopted by the CDU (East) and pastors close to the Pfarrerbund (dissolved since 1974), which brackets the official ideology as unacceptable, but fully embraces the government's practical policies. These socialist Christians, Falcke explains, distinguish between salvation (*Heil*) and social well-being (*Wohl*) and claim that the gospel deals exclusively with salvation, while Marxism-Leninism as the science of society is the authoritative guide in matters dealing with people's well-being. For these socialist Christians, the gospel offers the forgiveness of sins to those who believe, but contains no message whatever in regard to the social order. Falcke passionately repudiates this radical separation of the personal from the social, and the spiritual from the material. Since the churches in East Germany had to deal with this topic in greater detail, we shall have occasion to return to it later.

Falcke mistrusts the cooperation of Christians in the GDR that is not at the same time the bearer of social criticism. He argues persuasively that theory and practice are never totally separable: human action always embodies in one way or another the vision of life that prompted it. When people guided by different visions work together in the same social project, their actions may look alike when seen from afar; but when examined more closely, they are bearers of different messages. They differ not only in the motivation that sustains them, but in the very meaning they incarnate. For this reason, Falcke argues, Christians may not naively and cheerfully collaborate with Marxist-Leninists, assigning their disagreement to the spiritual order. Christian cooperation with the socialism of the GDR bears within it a critical dimension derived from the gospel that demands frank and open acknowledgement. Cooperation and critique must go together. Falcke called this "critical solidarity." This term, we note, entered the discourse of the Kirchenbund.

Our comparison between the writings of Schönherr and Falcke has shown that the bold path between total surrender and total opposition was not a narrow ridge, but allowed for different options. As president of the Bund, Schönherr was responsible for preserving a consensus within the federation and negotiating with the government the conditions of a free social space for the Church. He walked the bold path by putting more stress on stable relations. More deeply involved in theoretical issues, Heino Falcke, teacher of theology, developed an understanding of cooperation that went hand in hand with public criticism. He walked the bold path in a more provocative way, often attracting the government's displeasure. Yet despite these differences, Schönherr and Falcke were friends and allies. Mutually supportive, they together served the Kirchenbund with their theological reflections.

CHAPTER 6

Barmen and Bonhoeffer's Radical Theology

What interests us in this book are the spiritual motives and theological ideas that guided the Protestant Church on its path through the GDR, acknowledging its location in the socialist society, forming a federation in order to exercise its mission more effectively, bargaining with the government for a free space to exercise its ministry, and entertaining the hope for a reformable socialism. Among the sources of the Kirchenbund's theology were the Barmen Declaration produced by the Confessing Church in 1934 and the theology of one of its architects, martyr of the German resistance, Dietrich Bonhoeffer.

*   *   *

The leading churchmen involved in the creation of the Kirchenbund had been members of the Confessing Church or were identified with its spirit. They always referred to Barmen as the starting point for a new understanding of the Protestant Church in Germany. The founding document of the Kirchenbund (art. 1,3) mentioned the Barmen Declaration and summoned the member churches to remain faithful to its spirit.[1]

1. Reinhard Henkys, *Bund der evangelischen Kirchen in der DDR. Dokumente zu seiner Entstehung* (Berlin: Eckart Verlag, 1970), 34.

Which elements of this Declaration were particularly important to the Protestant leaders in the GDR? The Declaration had been composed by the Confessing Church as a protest document against Hitler's successful attempt to invade the Protestant establishment, violate the Church's autonomy, and make its teaching correspond to National-Socialist racist ideology. The Declaration affirmed the Church's fidelity to Jesus Christ alone and his dominion over every aspect of human life. Yet Christians who had actively resisted National-Socialism, Albrecht Schönherr among them, felt that the Barmen Declaration had actually been a weak document, lacking courage: it only opposed Hitler's violation of the Church's autonomy and had nothing to say regarding his violation of human rights, the persecution of the Jews, the philosophy of German superiority, and the preparation for a world war. Still, in the history of German Lutheranism, which was traditionally supportive of the state, Barmen was a major event and a turning point. It became the rallying-point of the German churches after 1945, especially among Christians who wanted to rethink the church's role in society and make an entirely new beginning.

Let us look at the elements of the Barmen Declaration that were so important for the churchmen in Communist East Germany. Thesis I had a Barthian ring: it affirmed that Jesus Christ, as witnessed in the Scriptures, is the one Word of God the church must hear, obey, and trust in life and in death. The church must resist any voice that interferes with its fidelity to Christ and Christ alone. This *solus Christus* emphasis is echoed in the Protestant theology in the GDR.

Thesis II had an immediate relevance for Christians in the GDR. Here is the text:

> We reject the false doctrine that there are areas of our life in which we would not belong to Jesus Christ, but to other lords — areas in which we do not need justification and sanctification through him. Thesis II: As Jesus Christ is the declaration of the forgiveness of all our sins, so in the same way and with the same seriousness, he is also God's mighty claim upon our whole life. Through him befalls us a joyful liberation from the godless fetters of this world to a free, grateful service to his creatures.[2]

2. Robert T. Osborn, *The Barmen Declaration as a Paradigm for a Theology of the American Church* (Lewiston, NY: Edwin Mellen Press, 1991), 19. All quotations

That there are no areas in human life that do not belong to Christ and are not under his rule was a message that was applied by Christians in the GDR to gain a positive approach to the society in which they lived. They acknowledged God's mighty claim on the whole of their lives, including their interaction with the socialist society. When bishops, pastors, and theologians emphasized that there were no blank spots or empty spaces on God's geographical map, they repeatedly referred to Barmen II. In its name they warned Christians against the temptation to bracket their own society, live emotionally in the liberal society of West Germany, or seek refuge in a spiritual withdrawal from their historical context.

Barmen II, one has to admit, can be interpreted more modestly. It only affirmed that there were no areas in "our lives" that did not belong to Christ and that God's mighty claim was upon "our whole lives," including therefore "our" social involvement. If the word "our" here refers only to Christians — which I think it does — then Barmen II does not fully proclaim Christ's sovereignty over the world. Yet the theologians in the GDR followed a stronger reading of Barmen II: for them it was a confession of God's mighty claim on the whole world.

Barmen II also helped these Christians to think of their church as a community of witness and service. Christ, according to Barmen II, liberates the faithful from the paralyzing fetters of the past and empowers them to offer a joyful service to their community, in fact to all of God's creatures. When Schönherr, Falcke, and the Synods of the Kirchenbund proclaimed that Jesus liberated his followers to assume responsibility in society and adopt an attitude of critical solidarity, they believed their message was faithful to Barmen II. In its name they rejected an individualistic interpretation of the gospel that would allow Christians to focus on their private justification and sanctification as if their daily interaction with society was not in need of salvation. Replying to the challenge of No Other Gospel, an evangelical movement in the West German Churches protesting against Bultmann's existentialist hermeneutics, Heino Falcke remarked that No Other Gospel was theologically sound only if its proponents applied the biblical message of sin and forgiveness also to their

---

from the Barmen Declaration are taken from this translation. Subsequent references will be given parenthetically in the text.

implication in the social reality.[3] Barmen II, read in the GDR, summoned Christians to take with utmost seriousness their involvement in the socialist society and to stand in solidarity with their secular co-citizens who wanted to improve justice and equality in their country.

Thesis III of the Barmen Declaration rejected "the false doctrine that the Church be permitted to abandon the form of its message and order to its own pleasure or to changes in political persuasion" and affirmed that the Church "must testify with its faith, its obedience, its message and its order . . . that it is God's property alone and lives and may live only by his care" (Osborn, 20). When churchmen in the GDR stressed the unbridgeable gulf between Christian faith and socialist ideology, they saw themselves as faithful to Barmen III. They rejected the idea of a Christian socialism, a socialist theology, and a fortiori a socialist church, because such an attempt of assimilation to the reigning ideology would compromise the Church's exclusive reliance upon Jesus Christ and thus be in contradiction with Barmen III.

Barmen was important for the Protestant Church in the GDR for another reason. Because the Christians who had signed the Barmen Declaration belonged to different regional churches — Lutheran, Reformed, and United — Barmen was a symbol of Protestant unity. For historical reasons going back to the Reformation in the 16th century, German Protestants deeply attached to confessional and regional traditions found it very difficult to move toward more united ecclesiastical structures.[4] Since the Kirchenbund in the GDR sought to foster the formation of a more truly united Protestant Church, church leaders reminded the local congregations, referring to Barmen I, that Jesus Christ alone — not confessions nor regional traditions — was the ultimate norm of the church's life. They also invoked Barmen III to show that fidelity to Christ demanded expression not only in the church's proclamation, but also in its "order," that is to say its self-organization. The church is held to proclaim the Good News even by its structure. In May of 1984, commemorating the Barmen Declaration after forty

3. Heino Falcke, *Mit Gott Schritt halten. Reden und Aufsätze* (Berlin: Wichern-Verlag, 1986), 19.

4. Manfred Stolpe, *Den Menschen Hoffnung geben. Reden, Aufsätze, Interviews* (Berlin: Wichern-Verlag, 1991), 76-80.

years, two Protestant bishops, one from the Bund, the other from the EKD, wrote a joint letter to the local congregations on the need for greater unity among them.[5] In the same month, Manfred Stolpe gave a speech in Berlin on the relevance of Barmen III for the search of greater unity among the federated churches of the GDR.[6]

Thesis V of the Barmen Declaration repeated the proscription against integrating the Christian church — its message, theology, or organization — into a totalitarian system, and by implication into secular systems of any kind. Rejecting "the false doctrine that the state, over and beyond its special commission, should and could become the single and totalitarian order of human life" (Osborn, 21), Barmen V affirmed the perpetual nonintegration of the church and its message into the nation-state, its organization, and its political theory. Beyond the repudiation of totalitarianism, this thesis has been interpreted as the specifically Protestant message that the gospel is so uniquely true and different that it is forever at odds with what passes as human wisdom, and thus it calls for an abiding suspicion in regard to secular systems of any sort. Karl Barth had emphazised this aspect of Protestantism, and Bonhoeffer had echoed it in his own, original way. The Christian thinkers in the GDR, faithful to this tradition, retained a theological caution in regard to philosophy and social theory. The Good News could not be fitted into any secular system. While the gospel freed Christians to learn from the good ideas and the good practices they discovered in the world, it also demanded that they qualify these positive elements in the light of Christ and insert them in a critically amended form in the Christian perception of reality. There must be no intermingling of theology and philosophy. We shall return to this topic later.

*   *   *

Of great importance for Protestant theology in the former GDR was Dietrich Bonhoeffer, an original theologian and man of wisdom who stood close to Barmen, laid the foundation for a new approach to

5. *Gemeinsam unterwegs. Dokumente aus der Arbeit des BEK in der DDR* (Berlin: Evangelische Verlagsanstalt, 1989), 201-202.
6. Stolpe, 91-101.

theology, and resisted with all his being the dark realm of Nazi domination. For his part in the conspiracy to assassinate Hitler, he was
hanged as a traitor. While some Christians were still troubled by his
deed and wondered if it was consistent with his theology of peace and
justice, Christian theologians in the GDR greatly admired him. In the
culture of the GDR, defined as it was in antifascist terms, Bonhoeffer
had his place of honor.

More importantly, Bonhoeffer's theological reflections were a
source of inspiration for the leaders and thinkers of the Protestant
Church. Most of them had belonged to the Confessing Church, and
some of them had known Bonhoeffer personally. Schönherr had met
him and listened to his lectures; and he regarded him as a great teacher
who, through his writings, continued to exercise a profound influence
upon his life, thought, and ministry.

In this chapter I wish to show the impact of Bonhoeffer on
Protestant theology in the GDR. Albrecht Schönherr himself has given
addresses and lectures on the relevance of Bonhoeffer's thought for
Christians and the church as they have tried to find their way in the
socialist society. Schönherr's writings on Bonhoeffer are profound and
beautiful: they offer a pastoral-spiritual interpretation of the Lutheran
sage and martyr, without attempting to create a system of his thought.
It is a pity that these writings have not been translated into English.

First, I wish to discuss several themes of Bonhoeffer's work that
were particularly meaningful for the Protestant Church in the GDR,
and then I will offer some Catholic reflections on this great Protestant
theologian.[7]

Bonhoeffer believed that in his day the church was called to a
conversion. What had to take place was a radical rethinking of its
message and its presence in society. What was needed — using today's
language — was a paradigm shift. One dimension of this conversion
was recognizing the primacy of practice. "Too late have we learnt that

---

7. The quotations from Bonhoeffer are taken from Schönherr's *Horizont und
Mitte. Aufsätze, Vorträge, Reden, 1953-1977* (München: Chr. Kaiser Verlag, 1979) and
Abenteuer der Nachfolge. Reden und Aufsätze, 1978-1988 (Berlin: Wichern-Verlag,
1988), and given in my translation. References will be given parenthetically in the
text.

the origin of the deed is not thought, but the readiness to assume responsibility. . . . You will only think what you choose responsibly to do" (Schönherr, *Horizont und Mitte,* 105). The church's tradition has been too theoretical. The church trusted words: it believed it was faithful to Jesus when it proclaimed his message and reflected theologically on his teaching. But words communicate the gospel only if the speaker lives the gospel. Truth is first of all a practice. The church must announce the gospel in its public stance and action before it can credibly proclaim it in its public discourse.

Only Christians who resist Nazi domination, Bonhoeffer argued in the thirties, are able to give authentic witness to Jesus Christ. He said, "Only those who shout for the Jews may sing Gregorian chant."[8] He denied the legitimacy of the established Protestant churches and recognized the Confessing Church as the only legitimate *ecclesia* in Germany.

Bonhoeffer thought that the Protestant Church's inability to say No to Hitler revealed the problematic character of its entire past: its veneration of and obedience to the state, its support for the traditional class system, its resistance to social change, its indifference to the plight of workers and the poor, and its opposition to socialism and working class politics. Paralyzed by this tradition, the Church now found itself incapable of assuming a critical attitude toward the Third Reich. In 1947 — as we saw above — the Darmstadt Declaration of the Bruder-rat explored this Bonhoefferian theme.

The Church's failure, Bonhoeffer continued, was caused by its preoccupation with its institutional survival and well-being. The Church supported the state and the established order to protect its own inherited privileges and the power derived from its status in society. In a letter written while he was in prison, Bonhoeffer wrote this extraordinary sentence: "Our Church, which in these years has wrestled only for its self-preservation as if this were its very purpose, is now incapable of becoming the medium of the reconciling and redeeming Word for human beings of the world" (Schönherr, *Horizont und Mitte,* 106). Bonhoeffer held that the Church no longer properly understood its own faith tradition.

8. Falcke, 17.

What was needed was a true conversion. To be faithful to Christ and Christ alone, the Church had to overcome its preoccupation with self-preservation and give up its former privilege and power. In doing so, Bonhoeffer believed, the Church would actually discover its real power, the power of the crucified and risen One, the power to stand in solidarity with the excluded, the poor, and the persecuted, to enter into their suffering, and to proclaim from this humble margin the limitless love and ultimate victory of Jesus Christ. The Church was not meant to promote its own well-being but that of others, especially those who have suffered harm.

This message inspired Schönherr and other church leaders in the GDR who, beginning in the fifties, tried to persuade the members of their churches that instead of resenting their loss of privilege and power in the socialist republic, they should embrace the historical situation as a spiritual opportunity to discover anew the meaning and power of the gospel. Inspired by Bonhoeffer, Schönherr kept on insisting that the Church should not be concerned with its own survival, but risk itself in the service of the wider community.

The conversion to which Bonhoeffer called the Church also had profound implications for the individual. If practice has primacy, if — in other words — action, or at least the willingness to act, must precede the utterance of truth, then the meaning of Christian faith has to be rethought. The Lutheran formula that Christians are saved by "faith alone," originally intended to overcome the Catholic emphasis on "faith and works," led to the idea that faith belonged to the realm of personal consciousness: belief in Christ's promise and awareness of being a forgiven sinner. Bonhoeffer argued passionately that this was not an adequate understanding of faith and justification. He accused Christians of the established middle classes (*das Bürgertum*) of holding a purely private notion of faith, one that did not alter their relationship to the social environment in which they lived. This sort of faith did not shake people's cultural presuppositions: it did not resituate them in regard to their own society. Christians could hold such a faith without questioning their position in the social order, without a commitment to justice, without the willingness to sacrifice their status and their privileges. If this concept of faith were true, Bonhoeffer argued in the thirties, then the Christians in Germany who compromised with Hitler would be, as they thought they were, authentic believers. But Bonhoeffer denied this. He called this concept of faith "cheap grace." In reality, God's grace was costly: it was both demanding and transforming.

Bonhoeffer is famous in the worldwide Christian community for having highlighted the concept of faith as discipleship (*Nachfolge*). Faith is the acceptance of Christ's call to become a disciple. Faith is therefore both a gift and a decision: it mediates a saving encounter with Jesus Christ; it implies trust in God and belief in God's message — all this is traditional. But faith here also means following Jesus. The Sermon on the Mount, the deeds of Jesus, and the way of the Cross here acquire a greater significance for the daily life of the Christian. Since Jesus had been at odds with his world, since he was inwardly free when others felt coerced, since he loved when others were selfish, since he was compassionate when others were hard-hearted, since he trusted when others despaired, since he embraced those whom the world despised and excluded, Christian believers now find themselves walking the same path, always failing, but always forgiven. Jesus, in the words of Bonhoeffer, was "the man for others," and thus by faith Christians and their church are also to be there for others.

The conversion to which Christ is calling Christians and their church has, according to Bonhoeffer, another dimension. Bonhoeffer belonged to the Christian theologians who believed that "modernity" — that is, scientific, technological, and democratic culture — had created a truly new historical situation, qualitatively different from the preceding phases of history, a situation that demanded a rethinking of the human vocation and therefore also a new manner of proclaiming the gospel. The world, Bonhoeffer argued, had reached maturity or become of age (*Mündigkeit*). By this he meant that in today's world, thanks to the development of science, technology, and rational administration, human beings were for the first time truly responsible for their collective existence. Their future was in their own hands. This did not mean, of course, that the modern world was better than pre-scientific societies. On the contrary, because the world had become of age, a new and terrifying possibility had emerged: human beings were now capable of destroying themselves and forever interrupting the human experiment. In the past, people were responsible for a certain sector of their world, possibly only for their family and their village. Now modernity had changed this: human self-responsibility now reaches beyond the traditional limits and embraces the whole of human life on this globe.

Some secular thinkers have revelled in this new situation. Humans, they argued, had become emancipated from the gods and discovered their destiny to create the world according to their own rationality. Christians, by contrast, tended to resist this concept of maturity. They believed that God was the author and ruler of the universe, that divine providence, not human planning, guided the course of history, and that modern men and women who claimed independent responsibility for the world were blown up by pride and blind to the many ways in which they remained dependent on God.

Bonhoeffer opposed any theology in which the affirmation of God's power implied that humans were weak and that therefore modern maturity was an expression of human hubris. He believed the church was blind if it refused to accept the modern perspective. In fact, in resisting modernity, the church was appealing to the worst inclination of the human heart, namely, to run away from responsibility. Bonhoeffer recognized that to become open to modernity was not an easy task for Christians: it demanded a total rethinking of what God, faith, and redemption meant. Christians, he argued, still use the inherited concepts; but they no longer have a clear idea of what they mean. They speak of salvation, and yet are not sure what this signifies. "The Church will have to find a new language that will be heard . . . , possibly an unreligious language that redeems and liberates like the language of Jesus" (Schönherr, *Horizont und Mitte*, 107). In this new theology, God will no longer be the heavenly Father, divine providence will no longer rule history, and people will no longer be children whose religious practices stand in the way of their secular engagement.

Yet what precisely this new theology will be, nobody can say. There may never again be a theology that thinks of itself as universally valid. Bonhoeffer made his contribution to the new discourse from his own historical perspective, realizing that in other parts of the world other theological discourses may well be required. For what counts in this new theology is not to define salvation, but to mediate it; not to explain justice, but to effect justice; not to disclose hidden truth, but to initiate transformation. Hence theology must be contextual, which means that in a modern society it must be comprehensible to secular people. If I may use a word commonly employed in contemporary theology, Bonhoeffer saw Christian theology as "a praxis," as theory that mediates liberating and reconciling action. Theology is to offer an interpretation of the biblical message that is grounded in discipleship and generates the practice of love and justice. Theology initiates a new perception of the world that prompts compassionate action and leads to society's eventual transformation.

An example of such a secular theology is Bonhoeffer's characterization of Jesus Christ as "the man for others." This term sums up the preaching and the life of Jesus; it also echoes Bonhoeffer's own attempts at discipleship, his public engagement for justice and peace and for people in trouble; and it summons forth a critical view of the Protestant Church (which was indifferent to others) and of National-Socialist German society (which was hostile to others.) At the same time, this secular discourse presents Jesus as the totally other, different from other human beings, who as sinners could never be there wholly for their neighbors. Jesus appeared here as the Transcendent, the Beyond in the midst of time.

Coming of age meant the entry of humans into total self-responsibility. Yet it also had another meaning for Bonhoeffer: it meant affirming "a single historical reality." This single reality is the earthly one to which humans belong and for which they are collectively responsible. Apart from this reality, there is no other world. There is no heaven and no cloister to which a Christian might escape to hide from this new responsibility. In his ardor, Bonhoeffer rejected all metaphysics, including a metaphysical God. There is no heavenly world. The Transcendent exists in the midst of history.

Bonhoeffer recognized, of course, that the Christian perception of "the one reality" is quite different from what secular persons see. The Christian believes that the living God is present in this worldly reality, present in the love of the neighbor and the care extended to the poor. This divine presence, Bonhoeffer held, was not confined to the church, but pervaded the whole of human history. Schönherr cited this bold and not quite clear quotation of Bonhoeffer:

> The total secular history is in reality already on the way toward being accepted and received by God in Jesus Christ. As in Christ the divine reality entered worldly history, so what is Christian (*das Christliche*) can only be found in the worldly, the supernatural in the natural, the sacred in the profane, the revelational in human reason. (Schönherr, *Horizont und Mitte*, 160)

Bonhoeffer believed that God was universally present in history, not as ruler from above, but as servant and healer. God was the gracious power that made people grow, assume responsibility for their social world, and reach out beyond the inherited boundaries to stand in solidarity with their neighbor in need. Bonhoeffer's prison friendship with Communists who loved their excluded neighbor and risked their lives in opposing Hitler (which few Christians did at the time) must have prompted this Lutheran theologian to say that Christ was redemptively present in the world beyond the borders of the church.

Bonhoeffer's theology of the one reality appealed to Christians in the GDR in dialogue with Marxism-Leninism. Yet in Bonhoeffer's thought there was, of course, no hint of an evolutionary drift in human history. God's gracious presence in history did not assure a progressive development toward a realm of justice and peace. As a Lutheran, Bonhoeffer's strong sense of sin protected him from indulging in evolutionary theories. While God's presence moved people to make the world into a place of justice and peace, human sin would continue to damage the world and inflict suffering on human beings.

An important theme in Bonhoeffer's writings — which I do not discuss here — was that God suffered with the victims of history and that the grace of discipleship included suffering with God or even, more mystically, participating in the divine suffering. That the suffering of others, especially the hungry, the exploited, and the persecuted, should occupy a central place in Christian consciousness is, I believe, a new development in the history of Christian spirituality. After Bonhoeffer, this spiritual message has received wide attention in all the Christian churches. Christians have learned to grieve over the suffering inflicted upon others by governments, economic institutions, and cultural forces in which they themselves are implicated and at the same time powerless to change.

Christians, Bonhoeffer held, must accept that they belong to this one historical reality, that they share with the rest of humanity the responsibility for the world, and that this is the context in which they must exercise their discipleship, walking the way of the Cross in freedom and paradoxically also in joy. Christians must open themselves to the issues that trouble their society, analyze the political situation and the economic conditions, bear the burden with those who are made to suffer, and struggle with others to make their world more just and compassionate. Responsibility, for Bonhoeffer, is a freedom granted to people — even if they should be secular — binding them to God and the neighbor. He believed that assuming this responsibility includes a surrender to God and the neighbor, even if the decisions that flow from it have to be made in the ambiguity and uncertainty of history. It is an anguishing task to decide what to do. Christians join their secular co-citizens in wrestling with this challenge, but when they make up their mind and act, each relying on his or her own judgement, each assuming his or her own responsibility, they need not fear — for they are justified by faith.

Christians realize that their historical situation is complex, that their analysis and evaluation may not be quite correct, and that by acting, they may unintentionally take guilt upon themselves. But because they have faith, they recognize that flight from the world is no longer acceptable. Assuming their responsibility, Bonhoeffer believed, they are justified by faith.

Despite his emphasis on practice, Bonhoeffer did not abandon the Lutheran doctrine of justification by faith alone. In a text quoted more than once by Albrecht Schönherr, Bonhoeffer recalls a conversation he had with a young French priest about how they saw their own lives. The priest had said that he desired to become a saint, to which Bonhoeffer replied that his desire was to learn to have faith. But upon reflection, Bonhoeffer asked, "What does learning to have faith mean?"

Later I became convinced and am convinced to this day that one only learns to have faith in the full secularity of life. When you totally renounce making something of yourself — be it a saint, a converted sinner, or a pastor — such renunciation I call secularity — then you live in the fullness of the tasks, challenges, successes, failures and confusions, then you throw yourself into God's arms, then you take seriously no longer your own suffering but God's suffering in the world, then you watch with Jesus in Gethsemane. This, I think, is faith; this is *metanoia*. This is how a person becomes a Christian. (Schönherr, *Abenteuer*, 45)

For Schönherr, Bonhoeffer's understanding of discipleship and justification by faith guides the Church in the GDR on the narrow path between total rejection and total assimilation. Discipleship demands that Christians examine their concrete social situations, criticize them from a commitment to love and justice, suffer with the excluded, yearn for a world more pleasing to God, and engage in responsible action to create a better society. Thus Christians approve of the humanistic ideals of socialism and have no desire to return to a free market society where human relations are determined by competition; but at the same time, Christians reject the government's official ideology and criticize the oppressive dimensions of the government's practical policies. Nevertheless, despite our yearning for a just and loving society, being finite, blind, and sinful, we may arrive at a false analysis or decide upon an action that may turn out to have been wrong. Still, having the faith not to run away from responsibility, not to defend ourselves by saying the wicked world can never be changed, not to invoke a divine providence that will take care of those who suffer, but instead to bear the burden of our complicity, to inform ourselves as best we can, and to act decisively and boldly, we shall be justified by God. The faith that we are sent by God and bound to act responsibly for the good of others is the faith that justifies, even if we become guilty in choosing badly.

Within this one, historical reality in which men and women exercised their responsibility, the Lutheran theologian sought to distinguish between two realms, "the ultimate" and "the penultimate," where the ultimate referred to the love of God and neighbor without limit, and the penultimate to the concrete strategies people adopt to express this love. The church's fidelity to the ultimate demands that it become a prophet in society. Individual Christians must go beyond prophecy, involve themselves in the penultimate, and cooperate with others — despite the risks — in the building of a just and peaceful society.

This theological argument for the church's narrow path between total repudiation and total surrender, we note, is different from the theology of shalom, derived from the WCC, proceeding from reflection on the creation, redemption, and sanctification of God's earth. We shall return to this topic later.

There are many reasons, then, why Bonhoeffer's theology appealed to Christians in the GDR. They appreciated what he had to say on the paradigm shift, the new historical situation, the primacy of practice, the church's conversion, and the need to give up its privileges, the gospel proclaimed in secular language, the role of political responsibility, and the solidarity with the poor. He was a guide on their path in the socialist society and enabled them to engage in critical dialogue with their Marxist co-citizens. Bonhoeffer even had a critique of religion — different, of course, from Marx's — but touching some of the same concerns.

Bonhoeffer was not the first theologian to distinguish between religion and Christian faith. For Karl Barth, religion represented the vain human effort of reaching out to God; whereas Christian faith was a gift, the result of God's gracious reaching out to human beings. The distinction between religion and faith is often used by theologians who live in situations where religion is part of a Christian culture and who therefore, as a corrective, stress the need for personal engagement and define Christian faith as repentance and conversion. For Bonhoeffer, religion belongs to the sacred space or heavenly world to which people can flee from their historical responsibility. Religion belongs to what Bonhoeffer calls metaphysics. It is other-worldly: it offers an illusory alternative to the one historical reality. Bonhoeffer's critique has a certain affinity with Marx's analysis of religion as escape, consolation, and illusion. By contrast, faith — for Bonhoeffer — is the call and acceptance of discipleship. Faith is secular: it summons the Christian to relentless responsibility for society.

It is possible to interpret Bonhoeffer's theology by paying exclusive attention to his emphasis on the this-worldliness or secularity of faith. Christian life is here simply "being for others." Yet this is not how Bonhoeffer was read in the GDR. There he was received as an orthodox theologian in the Lutheran tradition. Schönherr constantly pointed to the presence of paradox in Bonhoeffer's theology. He quoted Bonhoeffer's phrase that to be a Christian in today's world means two things, "prayer and doing justice" (Schönherr, *Horizont und Mitte,* 107). Bonhoeffer himself was a man of prayer. People who knew him well, even in prison, said that he constantly lived in God's presence. He also believed in resurrection. He spoke of death as "the highest feast on the way of freedom" (Schönherr, *Horizont und Mitte,* 132); and before his execution, he muttered that he was about to begin his real life. Schönherr insisted that Bonhoeffer cannot be accused of "horizontalism" since he recognized two dimensions in human history. Yet revealed in Christ — so Bonhoeffer — is that the "above" came from "below" (Schönherr, *Abenteuer,* 257).

Schönherr pointed to another paradox. While Bonhoeffer did not wish to think of Christian faith as religion, he criticized the individualism characteristic of liberal Protestantism; and following St. Paul, he spoke of Christ's presence in the body of the faithful. He defended the need for an organized church with its own legal structure because without such a structure the church would be unable to speak in the name of all its members and offer public witness in society, especially in moments of temptation and danger. When Hitler successfully invaded the Protestant Church in Germany, the protest of individual Christians would have had little symbolic power. What counted for Bonhoeffer was the setting up of a counter-structure, the Confessing Church, which presented itself as the only legitimate Protestant *ecclesia* in Germany. Christian faith, it would seem, called for organized religion.

Let me mention another paradox in Bonhoeffer's theology. He refused to speak of God as fulfilling human needs. Becoming of age, we recall, is the modern discovery that we are responsible for our lives in common and that if we have needs, we have to attend to them by ourselves. If God is defined as the fulfiller of human needs and desires, then the modern achievement of satisfying so many human yearnings leaves less and less space for God, until God disappears altogether. "God is no filler of gaps" is how Bonhoeffer puts it. At the same time, Bonhoeffer believes that the human project, the one reality for which people relying on their intelligence and good will assume responsibility, is constantly threatened by pride, greed, and the will to power. The human project is vulnerable to sin and easily becomes a self-destructive undertaking. What is needed — the word cannot be avoided — is

God's gift of freedom, the freedom to assume responsibility bonded to God and the neighbor. God may not be the satisfier of needs, but God graciously fulfills the one original need, restoring the lost freedom that enables humans to look after their needs in the plural.

*   *   *

Bonhoeffer's theology is full of paradoxes. The Lutheran tradition, if I understand it correctly, lends itself well to such a methodology. Here revealed truth is assimilated not so much by concepts in the mind, as by a redemptive passage from blindness to sight. Theology here does not aspire to constitute a coherent system of ideas, but rather tries to develop a discourse that questions people's perception of reality, makes them see their lives in a new light, and moves them to renew their dedication and act boldly. Bonhoeffer — and, after him, Schönherr — insist that Jesus Christ is not a principle or a set of ideas that has universal meaning and therefore reveals the truth of every particular. Christ's ethics are not a set of rules to be applied in every situation. They rather see Christ as a living person, God's creative and redemptive Word, engaged in dialogue with the church. They hold that from the ongoing encounter with this Christ, Christians in the church, taking their historical context seriously, learn what is to be believed and done. Truth is here always rescue from blindness; and goodness, release from paralysis. In this redemptive process, paradox may be more effective than the internal coherence of ideas.

As a Catholic theologian, I read Bonhoeffer with great admiration. He provides what Catholics call *lectio divina* or spiritual reading. Reading him I feel myself addressed, questioned, opened up, and confirmed. Yet reading his texts as theology raises a certain number of questions. Since Bonhoeffer's rhetoric pervades the Protestant theology of the GDR, I wish to make a few theological comments on his thought from a Catholic perspective.

The paradigm shift announced by Bonhoeffer has been accepted in one way or another by many Protestant and Catholic theologians. Repenting of the age-old identification with Western empire, recognizing the human vocation to be responsible for the world's future, acknowledging the primacy of practice, embracing universal solidarity, overcoming traditional theological dualism, and welcoming with wonder God's creative and redemptive presence in history — this shift of perspective has been adopted by many Catholic theologians and has already influenced the Catholic Church's official teaching. In Karl Rahner this new perspective is pursued in a liberal, humanistic setting; while in Johann-Baptist Metz — and more generally, in political and liberation theology — the same perspective is taken in a more radical setting, putting the accent on the preferential option for the poor. Catholics identified with this theological trend fully agree with Bonhoeffer that there is no alternative reality where people can find rescue from their collective responsibility for this world: with him, they also believe in prayer and resurrection.

What puzzles the Catholic reader of Bonhoeffer is his oft-repeated aversion to metaphysics. Schönherr and Falcke seem to follow him in this. Günter Jacob, in a book on the Christian life in the socialist society, offers an extended argument that in the world of science and technology there is no room for a metaphysical divinity.[9] These theologians are willing to live with the paradox of divine this-worldliness and life beyond death, without attempting to bring some sort of coherence to these two positions.

Why this suspicion of metaphysics? There is, first, the traditional Protestant rejection of metaphysics as an effort of human intelligence to move from the visible world to its invisible Author. Only through divine revelation, Protestants argue, are people delivered from their blindness and do they come to recognize God's presence in the world and God's plan for their lives. Still, classical Protestantism affirmed a biblical metaphysics — without necessarily using this term. Affirming the world as created is surely a metaphysical statement; that is, a trans-empirical statement that illumines the being of the visible world — even if it is not based on human reason, but on God's Word alone. The Bible is a metaphysical book in the sense that it makes believers recognize the world's origin and destiny. Did Bonhoeffer share this classical Protestant position? His statements — repeated with approval by Schönherr and Falcke — that Christ is at work in the world seem

---

9. Günter Jacob, *Der Christ in der sozialistischen Gesellschaft* (Stuttgart: Evangelische Verlagsanstalt, 1975).

to go beyond the classical Protestant position restricting Christ's grace to believers who know him *ex auditu,* from hearing the biblical message. But if God does take the initiative in people's lives, even if they are secular, why then should Bonhoeffer be so opposed to the idea that they, reflecting — with God's guidance — on the world of their experience, could acquire metaphysical insights? If grace precedes the recognition of truth, and if grace is offered in the world beyond the church, why should not people using their intelligence in a graced situation make important metaphysical discoveries?

Another reason why Bonhoeffer polemicized against metaphysics was that the very term suggested to him an alternative reality that allowed people to opt out of their responsibility for this world. People concerned with the metaphysical easily regard the physical as a lower order and thus refuse to take history seriously. The metaphysics of Plato was certainly dualistic in this sense. But already Aristotle tried to overcome this dualism, and even if he did not have the modern concept of history, he did see people located in society and their quest for truth and goodness as a spiritual way making them creators of a just and peace-loving, albeit non-egalitarian city-state. Metaphysics does not necessarily project an alternative reality. Certainly, Bonhoeffer's own biblical metaphysics, affirming God's gracious presence in history, was nondualistic, even if he believed in life eternal. Some theologians have read Hegel as a Christian philosopher who held that the Spirit was alive in the world and who proposed a metaphysics that accounted for the self-realization of humans in history. Certainly, Catholic theologians like Blondel and Rahner developed a metaphysical position, sometimes called panentheism, according to which God's sovereign transcendence was not over-and-against but in-and-through the world, graciously enlightening people to pass beyond their blindness to the truth, enabling them to move beyond self-concern to the love of neighbor, and opening them up to hope for the unexpected. In any case, the search for a nondualistic theology does not necessarily imply the rejection of metaphysics.

It is more likely that Bonhoeffer and his East German followers polemicized against metaphysics because they thought it did not respect the primacy of practice. Is it possible to acknowledge spiritual reality from any and every location in history? Or does openness to the spiritual dimension demand an antecedent commitment to love and justice? This is an issue that greatly concerns liberation theology. In Latin America, groups identified with the rich in situations of grave injustice often loudly proclaim their Christian faith and present themselves as protectors of Christianity. But is their God the God of the Bible? Or is their God an element of an ideology that protects their power and wealth? Can the existence of the true God be affirmed from any and every position in society? Liberation theology upholds the primacy of action. Like Bonhoeffer, it thinks of faith as discipleship. The preferential option for the poor is the only entry into the realm of the Spirit: without this option, there is only make-believe and illusion. Like Bonhoeffer, liberation theologians are suspicious of traditional metaphysics, because it presents itself as a wisdom available to all, whatever their social commitment.

Still, recognizing discipleship or the option for the poor as the first step, it is possible to make metaphysical affirmations as a second step. This is the solution offered by liberation theology. The praxis of faith sheds light on the one historical reality, making possible the knowledge of a depth dimension beyond its materiality. Why is this such an important issue? Because denying metaphysics in principle has been interpreted as saying that God, Christ, and salvation constitute a healing and liberating discourse without any reference to a trans-empirical order. Speaking of Jesus Christ is here only a way of saying that there is hope for the human project of building a world of freedom and love. There are theologians who hold this view:[10] it is sometimes called Christological atheism.

The tone of Bonhoeffer's deeply moving prose forbids such an interpretation. He lived and breathed in the invisible realm present in and through the empirical, historical reality. He praised God's active presence in the world. He was a metaphysician of faith.

10. Cf. Alfredo Fierro, *The Militant Gospel* (Maryknoll, NY: Orbis Books, 1977).

CHAPTER 7

The Doctrines of the Two Kingdoms and Christ's Kingship

The Kirchenbund included churches with different confessional traditions. A certain tension existed between the United Lutheran Churches (VELK), representing the Lutheran tradition in its purity, and the Protestant Church of the Union (EKU), representing an integration of Lutheran and Reformed traditions. The difference among the churches also reflected regional loyalties, a phenomenon related to Germany's feudal past. The conversation between Lutheran and Reformed theologians on the European level and the resulting Leuenberg Concord of 1974 stimulated the churches in the GDR to engage in ecumenical dialogue among themselves. In 1976 the VELK and the EKU in East Germany, both members of the Kirchenbund, created a theological commission to examine what light the new agreement shed on their different doctrinal legacies, especially the doctrine of the two kingdoms, held by the Lutherans, and the doctrine of Christ's kingship (of Calvinist origin), held by the Protestants of the Union. The commission was to study this matter by taking into account the particular situation of the Protestant Church in the GDR. The report of this commission moved Helmut Zeddies, a theologian working for the Kirchenbund's division of studies, to write a long essay tracing the use and meaning of these two doctrines in the short history of the East German Church.[1] This interesting essay analyzes the

---

1. *Gemeinsam unterwegs. Dokumente aus der Arbeit des BEK in der DDR* (Berlin: Evangelische Verlagsanstalt, 1989), 289-332.

103

theological wrestling taking place among Christians as they found their way in the socialist society.

*   *   *

The first ecclesiastical documents that sought a theological approach to the church's presence in the East German republic were two papers, one presented at the synod of the EKU in 1959, invoking Christ's universal kingship, and the other presented at the bishops' conference of the VELK, appealing to the doctrine of the two kingdoms. Against the fear Christians had of Communism and against their continued identification with West Germany, the first paper of the EKU proposed that in faith Christians must accept the socialist society as the place where they practice their obedience to God. The paper warned against two dangers: seeking refuge from society in interiority; and binding the gospel to any social system, be it liberal democracy or Marxist socialism. According to the paper, the relevance of God's Word is not confined to the church but addresses the whole of humanity.

The theological foundation offered by this paper was the message of God's kingship in Jesus Christ crucified and risen, reconciling the whole of sinful humanity. In Christ, God delivers humanity from sin and death — in fact, from all that is evil. Since Christ's victory is marked by his suffering and his cross, Christians may not misread his kingship in an enthusiastic or triumphalist fashion. Thus Christians may not argue that Christ's kingship demands the total repudiation of socialist society as if their faith is destined to conquer all unbelief in history. Nor may Christians use Christ's kingship to support a total surrender to socialism, arguing that Christ is at work in that society, atheist though it be. Christ's kingship reveals itself in an inevitably sinful world. At the same time, Christ's victory does not set a holy church against a sinful society, nor a holy society against unholy societies. Sin pervades them all. That is why Christians must reject the vocabulary of the Cold War. Christians may detect "the divine empowerment" or God's victory in the world wherever powers — people and their institutions — "promote life, justice and peace."[2] Even a state committed to an ideology

2. *Gemeinsam*, 292.

may become an instrument of God's life-promoting grace. Christians relate themselves to their society, not by a global acceptance or global rejection, but by a discernment of faith.

Zeddies points out that the paper presented to the EKU was also sensitive to the concern associated with the doctrine of the two kingdoms. According to the paper, the country to which Christians belong is the place where they obey God and where their faith is tested. Thus Christians belong to two distinct orders: one defined by acting responsibly in the world, and the other by clinging to God's Word in faith.

Moreover, warning against enthusiasm and triumphalism in the Christian approach to society, the paper recommended the use of reason in matters dealing with society, a point dear to upholders of the two-kingdom doctrine, which assigns reason to the worldly and faith to the divine order.

The second paper presented at the bishops' conference of the VELK in 1960 deals with the same issue: How shall Christians relate themselves to the new situation in the socialist society? This paper also opposes the attitude of Christians who refuse to accept the new conditions, continue to think of the undivided Germany as their true home, or live a life of faith as if society did not exist. Christians must find their way in the new situation in reliance on God's Word alone. Their attitude to the state, the paper set forth, must be derived from the biblical doctrine (Romans 13) that the state's authority is derived from God. The rule of government is a piece of God's rule over the world: it belongs to the wise and merciful ordinances of God, which are intended to tame and control a sinful world, and which "remain effective even where the people in charge are unaware of the origin of their power or misuse the authority with which God has entrusted them" (*Gemeinsam,* 294). Christians in the GDR are thus held to respect and obey their government.

The second paper refers specifically to the two-kingdoms doctrine of classical Lutheranism. God rules the world through two distinct regimes: first, through the ordinances of creation, including the state, keeping law and order in the society that remains, even after Christ's coming, the battleground of good and evil; and second, through the grace of Christ's redemption received in faith, initiating the believing community to the newness of life, to love, forgiveness, and peace. The worldly regime is temporal, awaiting its end on the last day of history; while the spiritual regime in the hearts of believers admits them to God's friendship and is therefore without end. In this regime of grace, the once-for-allness of Christ's salvific deed, the *solus Christus* and *sola gratia,* so dear to the Lutheran tradition, find their full meaning.

The practical conclusion that the second paper drew from the doctrine of the two kingdoms was that no state, no society, no economy, no philosophy, no reason could ever claim to be "Christian." The specifically Christian thing (*das Christliche*) belonged to the kingdom of grace. The paper recognized that in the past the two-kingdoms doctrine has often been used by the church to make people uncritical in regard to the state and to legitimate its policies. That is why the paper stressed that Christians, while respecting and obeying the state, must nonetheless be critical in regard to it and recognize the ways in which it violates God's intention for the world.

Christians must do their duty in the world: through their work, trade, or profession and their activities in society, they must serve the well-being of their fellow human beings. In this order, reason exercises its competence. But the activity and the ideas appropriate in this order do not communicate salvation; they do not mediate an encounter with the gracious God. But while the state is not intended to offer salvation, it moves against God's will when it becomes an obstacle to salvation, as in the GDR, where it promotes an atheistic ideology. The state here refuses to recognize its limits, it assumes the role of a religious authority, and it transcends its God-given authority and invades the realm of ultimacy from which it is excluded. In this situation, the paper concluded, Christians must respect and obey the socialist state in which they live; but because of its official atheism, they cannot become cooperators. They must do their daily work and be of service to their neighbor, but they may not cooperate with atheists in building an atheist society.

*   *   *

In 1963 the two churches in the GDR, EKU and VELK, decided to overcome their disagreement and formulate a common statement on the church's mission in the socialist society. This resulted in Ten Articles that were submitted to and eventually approved by all regional churches and the joint leadership conference. The Ten Articles avoided a direct reference to the two doctrines of Christ's kingship and the two kingdoms invoked in the previous papers. They made a new beginning by turning to Barmen as a source of theological inspiration. They affirmed that Jesus Christ has sent his church into world to proclaim God's reconciliation with all humans and to give witness to God's will in all areas of life. Christians must therefore examine the social conditions in which they live to discern what is the good God wants them to do there. Christians may therefore not interpret the given social conditions as an expression of the divine will, nor as a sign that God has deserted them. Since Christ is the decisive, even though hidden reality in the world's history, divine goodness supports and protects the humanity of men and women even in an atheist society. What is thus called for is a distinction between the church's divinely-demanded service that fosters life, and its divinely-demanded refusal to be bound to a socialist vision.

This distinction brought about a reconciliation between the two opposing theological trends. The Ten Articles recognized the divine empowerment to promote life, justice, and peace, confessed in the first paper on the basis of Christ's kingship, as well as the church's unwillingness to overlook the harm done to Christian faith by society's official atheism, expressed in the second paper on the basis of the doctrine of the two kingdoms. In the Ten Articles both are required: discriminating cooperation in the socialist society, and resistance to what offends the Christian conscience. The Ten Articles drew upon Barmen II, which proclaimed that Jesus Christ is God's mighty claim on our whole life, including the social and political area, and upon Barmen V, which rejected the false doctrine that the state may transcend its commission and become a spiritual guide.

The Ten Articles pointed the way in which the Kirchenbund was eventually to move. Yet another document, the Seven Theses of the Weissensee study circle, published soon after the Ten Articles, added a new dimension that was to be equally influential. In chapter 3 we discussed the theses proposed by Schönherr to the Weissensee study circle in 1960, which contained the statement that God's aim was not the church, but God's coming reign; not ecclesiastical existence, but the obedience of faith; not a self-satisfied community in a ghetto, but bold witnesses in society, even if it should be atheist (see pp. 31-32 above).

The Seven Theses of 1963 elaborated by the Weissensee study circle pursue this perspective further. They acknowledge Christ's decisive though hidden presence in the world's history; but they interpret this in terms of his service, not his victory. Not the risen Lord, but the humble Servant of God, crucified and vindicated, must become the starting point for the church's self-understanding. Jesus Christ, who emptied himself in the service of others, now empowers his church to forget itself in the service of society and to become solidary with the whole of humanity. The Weissensee theses clearly echo Dietrich Bonhoeffer's theology.

According to Weissensee, solidarity with the world means that the church in the GDR may no longer look upon society as godless and therefore abstain from social participation, selfishly worried about its own salvation. Freed by Jesus Christ, the church approaches the non-Christian society without fear or resentment, offering its service and its responsible, discerning cooperation. The church's vocation is to be there for others. Its relation to society is here defined in terms of nearness, not of distance, with an emphasis on participation, not on ecclesiastical autonomy. Weissensee can be read as opposing the two-kingdoms doctrine when it warns the Christian community not to look upon the world as the realm of law under God's judgment, and upon itself as the realm of grace under God's gracious call. For the truth is that in Christ, God has extended the call of grace to all human beings. Weissensee implicitly endorses the doctrine of Christ's kingship, re-interpreting it by defining Christ's rule in terms of service and sacrifice.

In his essay, Helmut Zeddies raises the question of whether this reinterpretation does not allow Christ's weakness and humiliation to overshadow his victory, thus leaving the world completely in the hands of sinful human beings (*Gemeinsam,* 300). Is there not a danger that if the church humbles itself and selflessly enters society, it may eventually cease to be altogether? Should not Christ's self-emptying be seen in tension with his final victory? In my own discussion of the Weissensee theses of 1960, I raised a similar question from a Catholic perspective, perplexed by — yet in admiration of — the Lutheran *solus* (see pp. 32-33 above).

The Ten Articles relying on Barmen, and the Weissensee theses echoing Bonhoeffer's theology, pointed the way the Kirchenbund was to take when it was founded in 1969. The Bund avoided direct references to the doctrines of Christ's kingship and the two kingdoms. Instead it referred to Barmen and preferred to use the terms and concepts worked out in the Ten Articles and the Weissensee theses. The Bund also recalled the 1947 Darmstadt Declaration calling upon the church to make a new beginning through conversion to God and a turn to the neighbor. The Bund, as we saw, defined itself as a community of witness and service in the socialist society. Following the Bishops' Letter from Lehnin (1968), the Bund recognized socialism as a more just form of human interaction. But in line with the Bishops Krusche, Schönherr, and others — we looked at the texts in chapter 4 — and with the Ten Articles, the Bund pursued the path between total rejection and total acceptance, refusing to say a global Yes or a global No to the socialism of the GDR, calling for cooperation in promoting life, justice, and peace and for resistance whenever the Christian conscience was offended.

The Bund even followed Bonhoeffer's concept of the "Church-for-others." In 1971 the Bund's Synod chose the Church-for-others as its theme and invited Bishop Heinrich Rathke to explain in a lecture what this concept meant. In line with Weissensee, Rathke argued that the church must not be from itself nor for itself, but allow God to be God by becoming the church for others, thus making present Christ's service in the world. As Christ was "the man for others" in total surrender, so the church must through its witness and service be "the church for others" without self-concern. The church takes seriously the *sola gratia* of justification only when it ceases to worry about itself. "The Church remains Church only when it is totally there for others" (*Gemeinsam*, 303). The church may thus not hide itself behind its walls, nor regard itself in pious arrogance as superior and distant. Still, while the church cannot exist without the others, it may not be *as* the others. For if it opportunistically chose assimilation, the church would lose its theological substance and cease to be church.

This warning against assimilation was a reply to participants who worried that the concept of the church for others did not sufficiently protect the church's distinct identity in the world. According to Rathke's presentation, the church is able to define itself as "being for others" only as long as it is faithful to the otherness of the gospel. With this clarification, the 1971 Synod decided to integrate this teaching into the Kirchenbund's self-understanding.

*   *   *

If theologians define the church's relation to society in terms derived from Christ's kingship understood as rule or as service, they are tempted to place many obligations on the church, multiply the "musts," and seemingly put the church in the realm under God's law. By contrast, the doctrine of the two kingdoms brought out the emphasis dear to Lutherans that the church was freely and undeservedly justified by its faith alone and hence no longer stood, as did the world, in the realm under God's law. While the Bund made no direct reference to either of the two doctrines, it vindicated the gratuity of salvation and the church's place in the realm of divine grace by a teaching, already mentioned in other contexts, on the church's freedom; that is, the freedom freely communicated to it by Christ.

The important text is the famous address of Heino Falcke, given at the Bund's Synod of 1972, entitled "Christ liberates — therefore the Church is for others."[3] This address, which has attracted our attention already several times, became an integrating element of the Kirchenbund's theological foundation. The text is divided into three parts: (i) Christ liberates human beings; (ii) Christ frees the church to become a servant for others; and (iii) the church's service serves human liberation. In chapter 5 we already saw Falcke's argument that because of Christ's gift of freedom to the church, Christians believe in a reformable church — and because of Christ's offer of freedom to humanity, Christians believe in a reformable socialism.

Looking more closely at Falcke's text, we now note that Christ touches and overcomes all human bondage at its root, reaching more deeply than any historical revolution in the name of freedom. Christ achieves this not only by joining the oppressed and discarded in his own humiliation, but also by taking upon himself the guilt and the

3. Heino Falcke, *Mit Gott Schritt halten. Reden und Aufsätze* (Berlin: Wichern-Verlag, 1986), 12-32.

punishment for the sins of selfishness, injustice, and contempt for others. Out of this bondage, which no human can escape, God has rescued us through the resurrection of Jesus, taking us with Jesus into the realm of freedom — a freedom destined to overcome the sin and slavery of the world, even though still marked by the shadow of the cross. The liberation brought by Christ, Falcke argues, enters in its own way in the contemporary, secular struggles for human freedom.

Christ frees Christian believers. First, Christ frees us for a life out of love freely received. The love of God poured forth in our hearts and confirmed by the love received from the community empowers us to become lovers ourselves. We are now able to act on behalf of others, especially the disadvantaged — not because we are obliged by the law, but because we love them. Second, Christ frees us to become of age. Following Bonhoeffer, Falcke interprets this as a freedom from fear and dependency that allows us to assume mature responsibility for ourselves and our place in society. This maturity does not encourage a "liberal" freedom of doing what we think is best for us, but rather a bonded freedom, born out of commitment to God and solidarity with others. Third, Christ frees us to be there for others. For Falcke, being for others means to follow Jesus in a love that transcends the boundaries set by the world, be they created by class, race, religion, ideology, success, or achievement.[4] Being for others also means solidarity with those who suffer. Here Falcke takes up a theme movingly developed by Bonhoeffer. But being for others also summons forth what Falcke calls a creative imagination inspired by love. Being for others means that we take their problems seriously, search with them for solutions, and relying on the Spirit, dare to propose alternative ways of organizing life.

This, incidentally, was a point made by Falcke in his arguments with the government which understood Christian cooperation simply as Christian motivation for doing what the government had decided. Since Christians are freed to have good ideas of their own, they want to be taken seriously and influence decisions made in the public realm.

4. Mentioning the overcoming of class hatred was taboo in the GDR. When the Catholic bishop of Berlin, Cardinal Bengsch, once — in a talk given in West Berlin — spoke of Christian love as overcoming race and class hatred, he was reprimanded by the government of the GDR.

Christ frees the Christian to live a life of discipleship. What Falcke hints at, but does not clearly say — if my reading is correct — is that the freedom for discipleship is identical with the freedom to believe and hence the gift of justification. This was Bonhoeffer's position also affirmed by Schönherr. The other, more common position is that the freedom to believe is the initiating gift that justified the sinner, and the freedom for discipleship is a gift subsequently granted. Bonhoeffer's position, it is my impression, was never universally received in the Kirchenbund.

Christ frees the individual Christian, but Christ also frees the church to be there for others. The witness and service the church is to render is not a series of "musts" assigned to it by law, but the fruit of the freedom freely communicated to it by Christ. To experience this freedom, Falcke says, the church must let go of its attachment to the past, its privileges and powers, as well as the piety and theological discourse inherited from an earlier period of its history. Thanks to this freedom, freely given, Christians trust that their church is reformable.

Being for others means that the church serves the liberation of humanity. In his controversial address, Falcke was bold enough to develop what this means in the socialist society of the GDR. We looked at this part of his address in chapter 5. There we noted that Falcke invoked the doctrines of the two kingdoms and Christ's kingship finding both useful theological models, each correcting possible false interpretations of the other. Yet, as we noted above, the Kirchenbund preferred not to refer to these doctrines at all. Following the Ten Articles of 1963, the Bund sidestepped the debate between the EKU and the VELK. The Bund defined its relation to society by drawing upon the theological positions of Bonhoeffer, Barmen, and Darmstadt; and in doing so, it received the support of all the member churches. This was a brilliant achievement. Since Weissensee proved to be an important source of inspiration, it is likely that this achievement was due to a large extent to Albrecht Schönherr, the Bonhoeffer student, theologian, architect of the Weissensee study circle, and eventually Bishop of Berlin-Brandenburg and the first president of the Kirchenbund.

*   *   *

Still, as we saw at the beginning of this chapter, the EKU and the VELK of East Germany set up a theological commission in 1976, after the Leuenberg Concord had reconciled the Reformed and Lutheran traditions in Europe, to study the two doctrines that divided them and come up with a proposal of how the two churches should relate themselves to this doctrinal difference. There is no need to give a detailed account of the commission's report. What it proposed was that the two theological paradigms, Christ's kingship and the two kingdoms, need not be understood as contraries and hence as irreconcilable; but they could be interpreted as complementary, each shedding light on an aspect of truth and protecting the other from ideological misuse. Each of the two doctrines summons Christians to responsible social engagement; and each calls them to a life of faith, trust, and thanksgiving, even if the doctrines offer different arguments for this call. Each doctrine has its strength and its weakness. Christ's kingship summons forth openness to the world and commitment to social justice, but it can also be badly used to justify the crusading spirit or Christian triumphalism, to offer ecstatic support for a political movement without attention to rational analysis, to bless the secularization of life and the loss of inwardness, or to defend an activist understanding of the gospel, forgetful of justification by faith. The two-kingdoms doctrine calls upon Christians to keep in mind the once-for-allness of Christ's salvific deed and joyfully live in his kingdom as forgiven sinners. At the same time, it summons Christians to do their duty in the worldly kingdom, which includes social responsibility, exercised soberly, relying on scientific knowledge without utopian expectations. Yet the same doctrine can be badly used to foster a self-righteous spirit of Christian superiority, to encourage indifference to humanity beyond the church's borders, to persuade Christians that their main duty in society is to obey the state, or to legitimate pious withdrawal from the world altogether.

The commission recommended, therefore, that the two, now reconciled ecclesiastical bodies not abandon their doctrinal heritage, but rather find theological enrichment in reading the two doctrines as complementary. This is how Falcke read them in his address that we examined above. The commission concluded that in the GDR the two doctrines together call upon the church to offer its witness and service in the socialist society along the path between total refusal and total acceptance.

*   *   *

There existed in the East German Church a relatively small, yet significant group of ministers who disagreed with the policies of the Kirchenbund. We have already referred several times to the Pfarrerbund, the pastors' association, that brought together over a hundred Protestant ministers committed to SED socialism. These men supported the Communist government and defended its political positions before their fellow Christians with theological arguments drawn from the doctrine of the two kingdoms. While deeply committed to Christian faith, they accepted Marxism-Leninism as the science of society. They had their own review, called *Standpunkt,* in which they debated their theological ideas. Many of these pastors were associated in one way or another with the CDU (East), I want to discuss their interpretation of the two-kingdom doctrine to show the reader that there existed a group of socialist Christians in the GDR, supporters of and apologists for the Communist government, who saw it as their Christian duty to collaborate with the authorities and persuade the Protestant Church, especially the Kirchenbund, to drop its critical distance. They were not satisfied with critical solidarity.

If, after the collapse of Communism and the reunification of Germany, we look back to the years of the GDR and try to evaluate the role of the Protestant Church in it, it is important to recognize the presence of these socialist Christians and the Kirchenbund's sustained and unrelenting resistance to them.

While the socialist pastors were critical of the Kirchenbund, they were nonetheless pleased with what they regarded as its increasing openness to the socialist perspective. They interpreted the creation of the Bund, the organizational separation from the West German Church, the discernment of place as *Kirche im Sozialismus,* the Bund's support for the government's peace initiatives and its policy of coexistence, as well as the Bund's participation in the anti-racism program of the WCC, as signs that the churches in the GDR were moving in the right direction. In a declaration made in 1974 celebrating the 25th anniversary of the GDR, these "socialist citizens of Christian faith," as they called themselves, looked forward to the Church's increasing openness to the concretely existing socialism and the enhancement of ethico-political national unity under the leadership of the SED.[5]

What the socialist Christians disapproved of was the Bund's critical solidarity, the bold path between total rejection and total surrender, the discriminating cooperation from case to case. They argued in particular against Heino Falcke's address given at the Synod of 1972, even if they did not mention him by name. In an article published in *Standpunkt* in 1973, Carl Ordnung proposed that the specifically Christian mission is the proclamation of the gospel and the formation of the Christian community, which does not include the offering of Christian ideas, Christian counsels, or even less, Christian programs, to the civil government. This, Ordnung argued, does not mean withdrawal from responsibility for society. Christians exercise this responsibility by making use of the concepts and methods society provides for all of its citizens. Christians have nothing to add to this secular knowledge; instead, they have to learn from it. Since socialism, despite its vision of justice and peace, belongs not to the divine sphere, but to the earthly sphere of political rule and social responsibility, churchmen may not draw from the gospel counsels for the improvement of socialism. If the church chose to adopt this reformist stance, it would simply be repeating outmoded and irrelevant concepts derived from Western liberal society. The renewal of the Christian community can take place only when its members recognize themselves as socialist citizens and as such ask new questions and find new answers (*Gemeinsam*, 312).

An article by Hartmut Bock, written in the same year, examines the contemporary meaning of the doctrines of Christ's kingship and the two kingdoms.[6] He recognizes that these doctrines have proven themselves fruitful for the church, even if they were occasionally misused for political purposes. At Barmen, Christ's kingship enabled the church to say a powerful word against fascism, but today the same doctrine is being used by the churches in Western liberal society to oppose the advance of socialism. Bock is critical of the WCC, which believes in the relevance of the gospel for Third World liberation and refuses to recognize that only

5. "Dieser Weg ist auch der unsere," *Standpunkt* (October 1974): 197.
6. Hartmund Bock, "Königsherrschaft Christi und Zweireichenlehre," *Standpunkt* (May 1973): 119-120.

political revolution can bring the solution. Today it is necessary to rethink the two doctrines from the standpoint of the new social condition and its spiritual structures. The two-kingdom doctrine is here of special relevance since it helps Christians to recognize that socialism is a this-worldly, secular reality that must be understood in scientific terms as a socio-political development following the objective laws of human history. Theological reflection is here only required to warn Christians against accepting these laws simply for reasons of opportunistic assimilation. Christians must learn that what guides socialism is scientific rationality: it has nothing to do with justification and sanctification in Jesus Christ. Bock was not sensitive to a point made by holders of the two-kingdom doctrine in the Kirchenbund, namely, the duty of the state to restrict its power to the secular sphere and not offer an ideology such as atheism that interfered with people's religious convictions.

Hartmut Bock argues against theologians in the Kirchenbund who use the doctrine of Christ's kingship to recover what he thinks they regard as the lost unity or coherence between the political and spiritual spheres. The new theology of liberation through Christ is, for Bock, largely an effort of the liberal-imperialistic ideology to respond to the growing power of socialism in the world. The coherence of the political and the spiritual, he argues, can only be found if the objective laws of history are accepted as scientific truth. Since there exists no interpretation of Christ's kingship unrelated to socio-ideological conditions, Christians can never use this doctrine to speak, as it were, from above to their political situation. At the same time, it would be fruitful for socialist Christians to explore the meaning of Christ's kingship from within their socialist commitment.

The relationship between human well-being (*Wohl*) and salvation (*Heil*) has become an important topic in Protestant and Catholic theology. For Falcke, as we saw in chapter 5, the two realms of secular justice and divine salvation were interrelated, because Christ's salvific deed promised humans rescue from condemnation, sin, and all the enemies of life, including oppression, as well as their ultimate reconciliation that could never be realized in history. This was a position congenial to the theology of the Kirchenbund.

In an article in *Standpunkt,* Gerhard Bassarak offers theological reflections on the relationship of well-being and salvation from a socialist perspective.[7] The two-kingdom doctrine, correctly under-stood, protects the church from understanding its mission to proclaim Jesus Christ as an entitlement to exercise a guardianship over the world. The poverty and human misery to which the church of the past responded with its ministry of charity has been overcome in socialist society. This does not mean that socialism offers salvation; it means rather that socialism frees the church for its specifically Chris-tian task, to proclaim salvation to the world. This divine mission offers the church no basis for claiming certain rights in society or for proposing social aims to society. In fact, by moving in this direction, the church would become an element of the world, set under God's law. The purity of the gospel, demanded by the Reformation, protects the church from moving beyond its sphere of competence. Not only the teaching of Marx, Engels, and Lenin, but the gospel itself denies the church the right to interfere in a socialist society. The two-king-dom doctrine makes the church realize that in the earthly realm, ruled by God "with his left hand" — Bassarak is here citing Luther — society is guided by human reason and competent authority, not divine revelation.

The separation of well-being and salvation does not mean that the two are not related. In socialism, people's material and humanistic well-being is the aim and purpose of society. In this society, citizens, including Christians, are truly at home. "We have had the best expe-rience with socialism as a rational and humanistic social order that discussions in the church should not question . . . with critical catego-ries derived from the Gospel" (Bassarak, 203). Christians realize that justification freely given by Christ moves them to do good, which in socialism means participating in society in serving the well-being of all. Justification does not create a distance from society, as is the case in capitalist society, but on the contrary encourages integration. The recent effort to expand the notion of salvation by identifying it with God's shalom is confusing (Bassarak, 205). A rhetoric of totality here leads to a loss of clarity. Salvation happens without human cooperation, while social well-being, though also God's work, takes place only with human

7. Gerhard Bassarak, "Heil heute und Wohl des Menschen," *Standpunkt* (Oc-tober 1974): 201-207. Subsequent references will be given parenthetically in the text.

cooperation. Salvation and social well-being are reconciled only in the lives of socialist citizens of Christian faith — and nowhere else.

With their "global Yes" to the existing socialism, Ordnung, Bock, and Bassarak were at odds with the basic orientation of the Kirchenbund and the theologians associated with it. The three socialist theologians rejected Falcke's use of Christ's kingship, the Bund's claim of Christ's universal relevance, and the ecumenical theology of God's shalom. They used the two-kingdom doctrine in a manner that differed from the recommendation of the commission set up by the EKU and VELK, which, as we saw, understood this doctrine as in line with the Bund's theological orientation.

When the Synod of 1980 insisted on the autonomy of the church and presented the relation between church and state as a partnership, the socialist theologians, Günter Wirth and Manfred Haustein, raised their voices in criticism (*Gemeinsam,* 315-316). They argued that the separation of church and state and the neat distinction of spheres recognized by the church leadership in the conversation with Honecker on March 6, 1978, implied that the church was in no sense a political institution. To claim spiritual autonomy and independence from the government is justifiable only as long as the church's concrete presence in society respects the principles and guidelines of the government. But if the church calls itself autonomous and at the same time a partner of the state, standing as an equal before the state, the church transforms itself into a political entity and betrays the agreement of March 6, 1978.

The truth present in this accusation was that a Marxist-Leninist state could admit no partner within its own society. The free space the Protestant Church sought for itself and to some extent obtained, was a contradiction within the totalitarian regime. It could not be theoretically justified from a Marxist-Leninist perspective. The government granted it, as we saw, for pragmatic reasons — because it desired the loyalty of Protestant Christians, because it wanted to foster social peace, because the Church supported by West German funds was an important source of Western currency, and because it did not wish to appear before Western observers as the persecutor of Christians.

The two socialist theologians, Wirth and Haustein, claimed that behind the Church's quest for a free space and the new discourse of partnership stood the age-old desire for ecclesiastical power, at odds with Scripture and presently anachronistic. The Church disguised this desire for power by a discourse of servanthood and expressions such the Church-for-others. The Church, the socialist theologians argued, wanted to influence the world: it produced its own social ethics to impose it upon society. But in pursuing this path, the Church left its biblical ground and betrayed the Lutheran tradition.

Already in 1977, Günter Jacob replied to these accusations raised against the theology of the Kirchenbund. His book carried the subtitle, "Against a False Doctrine of the Two Kingdoms."[8] This doctrine becomes false, he argues, when it is used, as it often has been, to legitimate the existing state, to protect it from criticism, and to promote political conformism. The doctrine becomes false, moreover, when it limits Christian faith to the private relationship to God and denies its relevance to the building of a just society. The indispensable distinction between the two spheres, the realm of the world and the realm of Christ's grace, is always in danger of being interpreted as a separation. Such a false separation occurs when theologians affirm that God is at work in history through supposedly objective laws that can be known scientifically and that operate in a deterministic fashion, and then are forced to conclude that Christian faith, hope, and love have nothing to do with shaping the society of the future. Jacob published his book in West Germany, for such an open and unguarded criticism of authors defending the official ideology could not be published at that time in the GDR.

The Bund, as we saw, preferred not to refer its theology to the doctrines of Christ's kingship and the two kingdoms. It invoked instead the Barmen Declaration, which affirmed the relevance of Christ for the whole of human life. Rejecting both the Cold War rhetoric of certain Christian circles and the socialist rhetoric of the Pfarrerbund, the Kirchenbund remained faithfully on the path of critical solidarity between a global No and a global Yes to the socialist society.

8. Günter Jacob, *Weltwirklichkeit und Christusglaube* (Stuttgart: Evangelische Verlagsanstalt, 1977).

CHAPTER 8

The Ecumenical Connection

"The Ecumenical Connection Enriches Us" was the title of the address given by Bishop Schönherr to the central committee of the World Council of Churches (WCC), meeting in Dresden in 1981.[1] To enhance the international reputation of the GDR, the government approved of the Protestant Church's participation at the Geneva-based WCC, gave permission for delegates to travel to international ecumenical meetings, and after March 6, 1978, even allowed such meetings to take place in the GDR. Schönherr explained to his audience how much the ecumenical connection meant to the East German Church. While the creation of the Kirchenbund in 1969 was necessary for pastoral reasons and as a response to political conditions, it also produced a certain sadness: it meant separation from the wider German Church (EKD) and enclosure in the borders of a small country. In this situation the relationship to the WCC offered East German Christians an opening to the worldwide Christian community, taught them to take seriously the challenge of Third World poverty and oppression, and made them recognize the Christian responsibility for "*das Ganze,*" the destiny of humanity and the earth.

To study the impact of ecumenical thinking on Protestant theology in the GDR and, conversely, the contribution made by the East

---

1. Albrecht Schönherr, *Abenteuer der Nachfolge. Reden und Aufsätze, 1978-1988* (Berlin: Wichern-Verlag, 1988), 66-69.

German Church to the WCC would be a major undertaking. What I wish to do in this chapter is simply to single out certain ecumenical themes that influenced Protestant thinking in the GDR and affected the orientation of the Kirchenbund.

*   *   *

In his book, *Gemeindeerneuerung,* Roland Degen examines the effort of the East German Church to renew the life of the local congregations. During the fifties, as we already mentioned, many Christians still had their hearts in the undivided Germany. Degen recalls that in 1954, Bishop Otto Dibelius, then president of the EKD, greeted the Kirchentag, the yearly national church gathering, with the exclamation, modified from Jeremiah 22:29, "O land, land, German land, hear the Word of the Lord."[2] For Dibelius, to be Christian meant not to give up on this German land; but for certain Christians in the GDR, this discourse was beginning to be unacceptable. Linking German and Christian so closely made them uncomfortable, because it reminded them of the German Christian movement that had successfully invaded the church under Hitler. In the late fifties, as we saw above, a new sense of pastoral responsibility emerged among theologians in the GDR, moving them to reflect theologically on their historical location. They called this *Ortsbestimmung.* This effort gave rise to a new approach to the church's pastoral ministry and new ideas regarding the renewal of the local congregations.

According to Degen's study, this new approach was strongly influenced by ecumenical developments at the WCC and the International Missionary Council (IMC). In the early fifties, wrestling with the increasing secularization of Western society and at the same time confronted by the resistance to Christian missions in the colonized or formerly colonized world of Asia and Africa, the IMC, ready to listen to radical thought, invited theologians to come up with new ideas. Among the theologians mentioned by Degen, J. C. Hoekendijk was the most daring and the most influential. In an article that had already

---

2. Roland Degen, *Gemeindeerneuerung als gemeinpädagogische Aufgabe* (Münster/Berlin: Comenius-Institut, 1992), 13.

been published in 1950,[3] he proposed several concepts that retained their relevance in the ecumenical movement and that had a special appeal for Christians in the GDR.

Hoekendijk argued that the missionary activity of the past sought to extend or restore the *corpus christianorum,* the stable Christian society, in which the church had enjoyed power and prestige (Hoekendijk, 15). Yet the Constantinian age has now come to an end, in part because of the irreversible secularization of industrial society and in part because Asia and Africa reject the church as a colonizing agency. Rereading the Scripture, Hoekendijk argued, we recognize Jesus as the eschatological messenger announcing the coming of God's kingdom. The aim of Jesus' mission and the church's evangelization is more than the salvation of individuals; it is rather the establishment of "shalom": the reign of peace, community, harmony, and justice (Hoekendijk, 21). This evangelization is exercised by the church through the threefold ministry of kerygma, koinonia, and diakonia, where kerygma proclaims the promised shalom, koinonia manifests the presence of shalom in history, and diakonia translates shalom into humble service offered to the troubled and disadvantaged. But if mission is defined in terms of kerygma, koinonia, and diakonia, then the church is by its very nature in a permanent state of mission. The church is not supporting missions as part of its many activities, but the church, properly speaking, *is* mission. Every single aspect of its life serves the redemption, reconciliation, and pacification of God's sinful humanity.

The mistake of the past has been a church-centered understanding of evangelization. Here the effort was to convert people to the gospel and make them members of the Christian church. Today, Hoekendijk argued, evangelization must be understood as kingdom-centered, which means that it serves God's approaching reign and assists the establishment of shalom (Hoekendijk, 40). The church proclaims Jesus

---

3. J. C. Hoekendijk's article, "The Call to Evangelism," published in *International Review of Missions,* April 1950, became available as a chapter in his book, written in Dutch, published in 1964. The German translation, cited several times by R. Degen and W. Krusche, was available in the same year; but the English translation, under the title *The Church Inside Out* (Philadelphia: Westminster), came out only in 1966. Subsequent references to *The Church Inside Out* are given parenthetically in the text.

Christ, not to increase its membership or extend its borders, but simply to give public witness to the promised reconciliation. The Spirit may use this proclamation to bring people to Christian faith, but this is not what the church aims at. In this post-Christian, post-bourgeois, post-religious world, the church can give witness to Christ only if it empties itself and is willing to die to itself in order to serve and enter into solidarity with the world (Hoekendijk, 47). The church willingly assumes the risk of losing itself in secular service because it trusts the promise of Christ that in so doing, it will actually find its life and thrive.

Hoekendijk and other similar voices influenced the assembly of the IMC held in 1952 at Willingen in West Germany. This assembly adopted the concept of *missio Dei,* according to which God sent his Son and his Spirit to redeem and sanctify the world; and the church's task of evangelization is to serve this divine mission.[4] Mission is here, in the first instance, God's. Hoekendijk and others interpreted the *missio Dei* concept as the recognition of God's gratuitous reconciling activity in history, mediated by the church, but not only by the church. Other forces in history, possibly even secular men and women, were, unbeknownst to themselves, servants of the divine mission and instruments of human reconciliation in peace and justice.

This radical interpretation of the *missio Dei* concept assumed that God was redemptively at work even among people who did not believe in Jesus Christ, the One Mediator between God and humanity. Protestants found this difficult to accept. Since Catholic theologians understand Christ's grace or God's saving presence in history in metaphysical terms, they do not find it so difficult to recognize the hidden *missio Dei* operating in humanity. But since Protestant theologians shy away from metaphysics, they hold that God's grace can only be received through a change of personal consciousness, that is to say through personal faith in Jesus Christ. For this reason the radical interpretation of the *missio Dei* greatly troubled the IMC, and later the WCC, and never received unanimous recognition.

---

4. Tom Stransky, "Missio Dei," in *Dictionary of the Ecumenical Movement* (Geneva: WCC Publications, 1991), 687-689.

*   *   *

While this new missionary theology was developed without attention to the situation of a church in a Communist society, it had an enormous appeal for Christians in the GDR, who were wrestling with a new understanding of their church's mission in society. The ecumenical missionary theology had an affinity with Stuttgart's hope for a new beginning, with Darmstadt's call for the church's conversion, with Bonhoeffer's church-for-others, and with Jacob's end of the Constantinian era. The new ecumenical theology encouraged the effort of East German theologians who were seeking to define the church as a community of witness and service in the socialist society. Even after the formation of the Bund, the ecumenical theology remained influential in the East German Church.

Already in 1963, the churches in the GDR created an ecumenical commission on the structure of the congregation, which was in constant contact with the WCC. Its president was Werner Krusche. In 1972 Bishop Krusche published his book, *Schritte und Markierungen,* a collection of papers, some dating from the early sixties, which discussed the new theology of mission proposed at the WCC (into which the IMC had been integrated in 1961). Krusche's main concern was the implication of the church's mission for the structure of the congregation. We shall see that while he was impressed by the *missio Dei* concept and learned from it — he often cited the work of Hoekendijk — Krusche tried to overcome what he regarded as its one-sidedness.

Thus while Krusche acknowledged that the church is essentially mission, he added that it is not only mission.[5] He agreed with the ecumenical theology that the time has come to give up the older idea of mission as preaching the gospel in foreign lands or charitable assistance to the underprivileged at home. And yet, since today's secular and unbelieving world tempts Christians to see themselves as a "little flock" or "holy remnant" and opt voluntarily for a ghetto existence, Krusche considered it of utmost importance that Christian congregations discover a more biblical sense of mission, extend their solidarity

5. Werner Krusche, *Schritte und Markierungen. Aufsätze und Vorträge zum Weg der Kirche* (Berlin: Evangelische Verlagsanstallt, 1972), 109.

to people in the world, and give public witness to the love and the promises of God.

We encounter among Christians two opposing views of the church's mission: the first one understands mission as the evangelization of unbelievers and the ingathering of humanity into the church; the second sees it as the universal proclamation of God's love through self-denying service, realization of God's shalom, and solidarity with the world in the hope of seeing breakthroughs of public reconciliation. Both views, Krusche says, are able to point to biblical foundations. Against a one-sided interpretation of the *missio Dei,* Krusche wants both views to be accepted simultaneously.[6] He argues that to extend solidarity to the world without the aim of saving people from God's wrath — that is, without intending to see them enter into the eschatological community of salvation — would not be an adequate testimony to God's love.

Still, assigning primacy to the *missio Dei* concept and transcending a church-centered understanding of mission, Krusche does concede that integration into the church is not the object of the church's mission: it is only its distant hope. The biblical doctrine of the final ingathering does not guide the church's missionary action, but only prepares the church for the great surprise. Secondly, the ingathering at the end may not be imagined in the church as it is presently structured. Even now, when people hearing the Word decide to become Christians, the church does not know whether the form of discipleship to which they are called can be fitted into the existing structures. Proclamation always creates something new: "*es wird immer andere Kirche*" (the church always becomes other). Therefore, if the church sees itself as serving God's mission, it must have flexible structures.

Krusche applies these reflections to the church in the GDR. How are its local congregations structured? He invites these congregations to examine their boundaries, the style of their worship, the discourse at their meetings, and the form of their religious instruction. Do these structures manifest the church's mission? In particular, Krusche asks, are these structures capable of receiving others? Would Marxists visiting a local congregation hear a message they understand? Or would they

6. Krusche, 114.

feel that they have entered a strange subculture? If congregations look upon the gospel as something to be shared, they must structure themselves accordingly. Already Barmen III, we recall, demanded — albeit in a different context — that the church's order or structure proclaim the Christian gospel. Krusche found that the local congregations in the GDR were too timid, too preoccupied with their own survival, too imprisoned in the inherited structures to be active participants in the *missio Dei*. He lamented the church's sociological captivity.

The ecumenical theology of the church's mission introduced the distinction between "go-structures" and "come-structures," where the former help parishioners to move into society, dialogue with other citizens, and be of service to those in need; and the latter help parishioners to sustain their community and deepen their contact with their spiritual roots. As always, Krusche wishes to avoid the one-sidedness found in some of the ecumenical study documents. In particular, he wishes to forestall the emphasis on "go-structures" leading to a neglect of the appropriate concern for the congregation and its spiritual life. *Sendung* (a German word for mission) and *Sammlung* (a German word for both ingathering and recollection) must go together. The Christian congregation can give public witness to Jesus Christ only if it is collected in unity and recollected in the Spirit. But if primacy is assigned to mission or *Sendung,* how can the congregation do justice to its community life and the cultivation of its faith? Krusche argues that these two concerns cannot be honored one after the other, nor one parallel with the other; for then community and spirituality would stand in the way of engagement in mission. What the church has to learn, he proposes, is to practice the kind of *Sammlung* (common worship, teaching, and pastoral care) that prompts and sustains *Sendung* (participation in the divine mission).

Krusche accepts the *missio Dei* theology proposed in the ecumenical literature with appropriate reservations. He acknowledges that the world, not the church, holds the center stage in God's redemptive mission; and he recognizes the signs of God's approaching reign in historical events beyond the church's borders; but he is not ready to embrace the theological thesis put forward in some ecumenical documents that Jesus Christ has revealed God's redemptive presence in the whole of humanity, graciously saving people for a new life of love. How

then does the church differ from the world? According to this thesis
— passionately defended by Karl Rahner and now widely held in
Catholic theology — the church remains distinct and set apart from
the world because in the church alone is Jesus Christ proclaimed and
celebrated. The church is the unique historical witness of God's universal redemptive presence. Krusche reports this theology in his study,
but does not endorse it.

His identification with the Lutheran tradition moves him to make
two critical remarks important for the church in the GDR. First, he
insists that the shalom of God can never be fully established in history
and hence that it always remains, even when a social struggle has
produced greater relative justice, a divinely proposed utopia exercising
a prophetic function in society. However just and humane a social
system may be, or intends to be, it can never be identified with God's
shalom. The anticipations of God's coming reign in history are always
fragmentary and vulnerable. We shall see further on how this idea was
developed in the East German Church of the eighties.

Second, Krusche offers a critical reflection on what the ecumenical
documents on the *missio Dei* call the church's "presence" in the world.
The church evangelizes, these documents say, by "being present" to
others, not by trying to convert them. Krusche objects to the strict
separation between presence and conversion. He shows that "the presence" of Christians, if taken seriously, implies a profound transformation of awareness. Christians are "present" to others when they listen
to them, understand them, learn from them, and even willingly share
their burden. But learning to be present in this way is not an entry
into assimilation, but a critical process in which dialogue with the gospel
plays an important part. Presence is not an uncritical surrender to
another cultural world, but a discerning process: discovering the many
voices in the other culture, including the critical voices and the cries
of those who carry the heaviest burden. Dialogue with "the others" may
therefore lead to a change of perception on their part. Conversely,
listening to "the others" makes Christians aware of their own short-
comings, their ambiguous heritage, and their compromised church. In
other words, "presence" calls for "conversion."

Since presence means not only understanding others, but also being
understood, Christians cannot be authentically present in secular society

without revealing themselves and giving witness to their faith. While this is done discreetly and nonaggressively, not aimed at converting others, it nonetheless shows that presence always includes proclamation.

The Protestant theology in the GDR, though radical and innovative, always remained in the orthodoxy of their church tradition.

*   *   *

Throughout its entire existence, the Kirchenbund retained a lively contact with the WCC. The interchange was mediated by an ecumenical commission appointed by the Bund. In Berlin there was also an Ecumenical Institute. The East German Church learned from the theological developments at the WCC, but it also made its own contribution to them in papers written by ecumenical commissions or individual theologians. Heino Falcke made several important speeches at World Council meetings.[7] In fact, the East German Church had a special place of honor at the WCC because it was the only member church located in a Communist country that was free enough to develop a creative theology of critical solidarity.

The Protestant Church in the GDR participated in the radicalization of the WCC that was produced by the impact of Third World liberation theologies, the international peace and disarmament movement, and the growing environmental concern in the developed nations of the West. In this evolution, the theological theme of God's shalom, proposed by Hoekendijk already in the fifties, became increasingly influential. God's shalom here referred to God's coming reign of peace, promised in the Old Testament and inaugurated in the New, that would rescue humanity from sin and all the evil forces that sought to destroy it. Shalom stood here for "justice, peace and the integrity of creation."

In this, the second part of this chapter I wish to recall the involvement of the East German Church in the "Conciliar Process for Justice, Peace and the Integrity of Creation" initiated and steered by the WCC, and the extraordinary impact that this ecclesiastical involvement had on the socialist society of the GDR. But before I turn to this event, I

---

7. Heino Falcke, *Mit Gott Schritt halten. Reden und Aufsätze* (Berlin: Wichern-Verlag, 1986), 231-264.

must say a few words about the changes taking place in the GDR in the eighties. When the build-up of nuclear weapons in Europe and the intensification of the arms race produced great fear in the two Germanies, the government of the GDR stepped up its support for the peace movement, accused the United States of aggressiveness and West Germany of compliance, and campaigned with the other Warsaw Pact nations for the removal of missiles in West Germany and a negotiated and supervised process of disarmament. The Protestant Church in the GDR offered its critical support for the peace policy of the government, even if its understanding of peace was much more encompassing. The Church criticized the government's campaign for peace because it put the unilateral blame for the arms race on the Western nations and created distorted images of the enemy (*Feindbilder*), both of which — the Church argued — encouraged the spirit of conflict and war.

At the same time a more radical peace movement emerged in the GDR that opposed nuclear weapons or even conventional weapons on principle and that advocated unconditional and unilateral disarmament. Similar movements existed in West Germany and other Western nations. In the GDR the radical movement organized itself in the church, that is to say in local congregations, in part because some of its members were Christians committed to God's shalom, and in part because there was no other space in that society where people could come together and raise their voices. The peace groups were not the only critical groups that were organized in the church during the eighties. Since the holding of assemblies and public criticism were forbidden by the government, people concerned with care for the environment, free artistic expression, and issues of personal lifestyle created groups in the local parishes. Some of their members were Christians; others were simply impressed by the Protestant Church's critical solidarity and its commitment to God's shalom, to justice, peace, and stewardship of creation.

These groups, including the radical peace movement, created certain difficulties for the Church. On the one hand, they took the Church's bold positions with utmost seriousness, complained that the congregations did not act in accordance with them, and urged the church leaders to live up to their own teaching and become more outspoken in their critique of the government. On the other hand, some of the congregations complained that these groups brought with them a secular spirit and paid little attention to the biblical message. The Kirchenbund itself was embarrassed because while these groups practiced critical solidarity and walked the bold path between total rejection and total acceptance, they were dissatisfied with the Church's polite discourse of dissent and preferred to be provocative and to challenge the government directly.

The radical peace movement, for instance, while faithful to the Church's theology, demanded on the practical level unilateral disarmament, which the Church did not, and sometimes even the withdrawal of Russian troops from the GDR. Since the agreement of March 6, 1978, had given the Church a free space to organize its own activities, the church leadership was worried that the provocative behavior of the groups might threaten the freedom for which they had worked so hard. Eventually the Bund appointed a commission, under the chairmanship of Heino Falcke, to study the critical groups in the churches and the problems raised by them, and to come up with a proposal of how the Church should react to this new challenge. To analyze the commission's report would take us too far afield.[8] In brief, the report recommended that while the Church did not "stand behind" all the positions adopted by these groups, the Church should "stand in front" of them, that is, take the risk of shielding them before the government. Why? Because of the affinity between the Church's vision and that of the groups, and because of the absence of a social space in the GDR for the free debate of common concerns. According to an oft-quoted sentence of Matthias Sens, "We discovered that they need one another: the churches the groups, and the groups the churches" (*Gemeinsam,* 272). Not until 1989 were the citizens' movements able to form their own independent organizations.

Toward the end of the eighties, the Conciliar Process in the GDR, in which all the churches were involved, including at the end even the Catholic Church, succeeded in mobilizing local congregations and critical groups in the name of God's shalom. The cooperative effort produced a remarkable theological document in the early part of 1989 and made a major contribution to the peaceful revolution in the fall of the same year.

8. The report can be found in *Gemeinsam unterwegs. Dokumente aus der Arbeit des BEK in der DDR* (Berlin: Evangelische Verlagsanstalt, 1989), 110-125. Subsequent references will be given parenthetically in the text.

What was the Conciliar Process? At the Vancouver Assembly of the WCC in 1983, the delegation of the East German Church, deeply troubled by the intensification of the arms race, proposed the holding of an international Christian peace council to warn the world of the imminent danger (*Gemeinsam,* 264). The East German delegation remembered that Dietrich Bonhoeffer had made an urgent appeal for a Christian peace conference at Fanö, Denmark, where he attended an ecumenical gathering in 1934. After Vancouver, the central committee of the WCC decided to summon the churches, not to a peace council, but to a conciliar process, a process that would involve the Christian people in their local congregations to discuss and define the meaning of "justice, peace and the integrity of creation" in their respective social contexts. It would eventually bring together the churches, each commissioned by its own people, to formulate and proclaim a common position on the meaning of God's shalom in today's world. The final event was to take place at the WCC Assembly in Seoul, Korea, in 1991. While the Conciliar Process was not a major public event in North America, in Europe, and more especially in the GDR, it mobilized vast numbers of Christians and had a considerable impact on public opinion. In the GDR, the extensive discussion of the topic in the local congregations and their churches over a two-year period was followed by three plenary sessions attended by elected or appointed delegates — at Dresden (February 1988), at Magdeburg (October 1988), and again at Dresden (April 1989) — which, taking account of the testimonies and submissions, elaborated a major document that was solemnly promulgated on April 30, 1989, in a worship service at Dresden's Kreuzkirche.

The Report, a substantial document of almost 200 pages in its published form, begins with a foundational chapter that explains the meaning of shalom in Old and New Testament and examines what conversion to this shalom would mean in the concrete situation of the GDR.[9] The subsequent chapters deal in considerable detail with issues

9. *Oekumenische Versammlung für Gerechtigkeit, Frieden und Bewahrung der Schöpfung,* Dresden-Magdeburg-Dresden, eine Dokumentation (Berlin: Aktion Sühnezeichen/Friedensdienste, 1990), 21-51. Subsequent references will be given parenthetically in the text.

of justice, peace, and environmental care on the local and the global level. What makes the Report a unique document is its frank and yet loyal critique of the existing socialism and its urgent call to conversion, for which there was no precedent in the GDR. No Christian theologian, not even the Kirchenbund, would have dared to publish this Report. In fact, the government urged the bishops to prevent its publication. But since the document was the result of a cooperative effort involving masses of people at the base over a period of three years, the government decided not to intervene.

The Report is an expression and a fruit of the Protestant theology in the GDR, even if churches that were not members of the Kirchenbund — the Catholic Church and several free Protestant churches, such as the Methodists and Adventists — also participated in the Conciliar Process and sent delegates to the assemblies. Still, the Report is in keeping with the Kirchenbund's critical solidarity: it follows the bold path between a global Yes and a global No to the existing socialism. The Report supports the humanistic ideals of socialism: it lauds the provision of people's basic needs — food, housing, and work — and does not recommend a return to privately owned means of production. The Report praises the measures taken by the government to assist the economic and political development of Third World countries, such as support for the New Economic Order and other proposals at the United Nations aimed at helping them, and the adoption of import and export structures at home that rendered useful services to the less developed nations (*Oekumenische*, 62-63). But the Report laments the government's opposition to any effort on the part of the people to improve or reform the socialist society (*Oekumenische*, 23, 85).

Under the heading, "More justice in the GDR," the Report describes the frustrations and the powerlessness of the citizens in that society (*Oekumenische*, 72-82). First, the ideological domination: the orthodoxy defined by the Communist Party, the absence of free discussion, the rejection of alternative socialist proposals, the suspicion that people are enemies of the state when they meet to discuss the future of socialism, the control of public information, the lack of transparency, and the rewarding of political conformity with career advancement. This strict ideological control, the Report says, is an obstacle to the reform of socialism.

Secondly, the Report describes the centralized control of the economy, the absence of participation in decision making, the lack of opportunity for personal initiative, the growing passivity among the people, and the waning of a mature sense of responsibility. Thirdly, the Report laments the orientation toward industrial productivity and the spreading consumer mentality present in the GDR, copied from the Western capitalist model, which have a destructive effect on the environment, nourish a new kind of selfishness, and produce a psychic indifference to the lot of others, especially peoples in the Third World. Fourthly, the Report finds fault with the forced cultural conformity in the GDR. Although men and women enjoy legal equality in the GDR, women have no social space to explore their own style and ideas; nor is there space for self-help organizations of marginal groups such as homosexuals, handicapped people, or alcoholics.

The Report was a theological document. The theology of God's shalom both provided the vision for society and generated the critique of present conditions. Moreover, the Report reveals the impact of the ecumenical movement on the Protestant theology in the GDR.

*   *   *

I cannot resist saying a few words about the important events that followed the Conciliar Process in the GDR, even if this history is beyond the scope of this book. The Report was made public in April 1989. Impatience with the government was growing in all parts of the GDR. The citizens' groups founded their own organizations, such as Neues Forum and Demokratie Jetzt. The great moment of mass resistance came at the end of September and the beginning of October. In all the cities of the GDR, people, deeply opposed to the dictatorship and the absence of dialogue, gathered in the churches, occupied the squares in front of them, marched through the streets in silence with candles in their hands, bold enough to risk being gunned down by the police and the army that surrounded them. So universal was this demonstration, so committed, mature, and peaceful, that the government gave in, granted the freedom of discussion, and joined the conversation at the round table.

Every city in East Germany remembers the dramatic events of the early days of October 1989. The tense confrontation between peaceful citizens and the armed forces in Leipzig became known internationally,[10] but similar confrontations took place in the other cities and towns, such as Berlin, Dresden, Erfurt, Halle, and Wittenberg. While it is not my intention to tell the exciting story of East Germany's nonviolent revolution, I wish to mention a moving incident that took place in the city of Dresden when people, tens of thousands of them, gathered at the station and the wide open space in front of it, interrupting trains and traffic. A committee of Protestant pastors and Catholic priests assumed leadership responsibility, calming the people over a public address system and negotiating with representatives of the authorities. The courageous Christof Ziemer, a leading Protestant pastor, played an important role here. At one tense moment, when negotiations with the authorities kept dragging on, a young Catholic priest took the microphone, calling upon the masses to signify their desire for a nonviolent resolution of the conflict, the people by sitting down on the ground and the soldiers by taking off their helmets. After a few moments of stunned silence, they complied, people and soldiers alike. When Lothar Kuczera, a Jesuit priest serving in Dresden, told me this story in the fall of 1992, three years after the event, he swallowed and had tears in his eyes.

In the weeks that followed, round table discussion took place everywhere. A journalist from West Germany, who had spent the last years in the GDR reporting on the growth of the critical movements, published the reports he had written over this period as a book entitled *The Protestant Revolution*.[11] Yet after the turning point, the Church ceased to play an important role. The citizens' movements supplied political leadership, and many pastors who had been involved in critical action left their ecclesiastical positions and became politicians.

Yet the sense of GDR-identity and the left-wing, democratic spirit that characterized the critical groups and the Church's contextual the-

10. *Leipzig im Oktober. Kirchen und alternative Gruppen im Umbruch der DDR* (Berlin: Wichern-Verlag, 1990).
11. Gerhard Rein, *Die Protestantische Revolution, 1987-1989* (Berlin: Wichern-Verlag, 1990).

ology did not survive for long. According to Friedrich Schorlemmer, the break between the idealistic critics and the people occurred already in November of 1989. A declaration spelling out the vision of a democratic, freedom-loving, socialist East Germany, a stable alternative to capitalist West Germany, signed by well-known activists, intellectuals, pastors, writers, and artists, was not well received by the public.[12] The attraction of the prosperous West German society was too great.

12. Friedrich Schorlemmer, *Worte öffnen Fäuste* (München: Kindler-Verlag, 1992), 302-306.

Conclusion

The path of the Protestant Church in Communist East Germany was altogether singular. We saw some of the reasons why this path had no parallel in the Soviet Union and the Soviet bloc countries. The GDR alone was of Protestant heritage. Even though the Protestant Church had come to represent only a minority in the country, it had the consciousness of having been the Volkskirche and hence as sharing responsibility for the people's well-being and having the right to speak out on issues concerning the common good. We saw, moreover, that the Church had a special reason to repent of the past and search for a new beginning. The Communist government, recognizing the uniqueness of the situation, did not follow the Soviet policy toward the Church, even though in other respects it faithfully imitated the Soviet Union. The government exerted various kinds of pressure on the Church, but it did not unleash a persecution, close ecclesiastical institutions, or arrest church leaders. Since public events in East Germany were keenly followed in West Germany, and since East Germany sought international recognition as a sovereign state, the East German government had political reasons for not persecuting the Church. Through its ecumenical connection, moreover, the Church could even help the GDR to gain international prestige.

In this situation the Protestant Church decided to find its own path in the socialist society: it created the Kirchenbund, which was independent of the West German Church and which strove to obtain

137

a free social space in the totalitarian state for its own pastoral activities. In the preceding chapters we have studied the theology that guided the Kirchenbund on its path of "critical solidarity" that rejected a global No and a global Yes to socialism and thus attracted the dissident groups eager to reform the socialist society.

What were the theological ideas and spiritual motives that influenced the decisions made by the church leaders? We noted first of all the Church's concern for its pastoral ministry: helping its members to live the Christian life in a new situation. We noted the Church's repentance over the German past and its own complicity, symbolized by the declarations of Stuttgart and Darmstadt that summoned the Church to make a new beginning. We noted the Church's position that the ethical ideals of socialism — cooperation, justice, and equality — were in keeping with the biblical promises, and that this humanistic project was not invalidated by the government's narrow, ideological interpretation of it. We noted the impact of the Barmen Declaration and Dietrich Bonhoeffer on the theology of the Kirchenbund, and the effort of the churches to find a common interpretation of the doctrines of Christ's kingship and the two kingdoms, an interpretation that would help them find their way in the socialist society. Finally, we saw the far-reaching influence of the ecumenical movement on the Protestant theology in the GDR.

The path chosen by the Kirchenbund was worked out and defended by three different, though interrelated theological themes. From the Barmen Declaration, echoing the voice of Karl Barth, was derived the theology of Christ's relevance for every area of human life. Christ, in whom God has claimed the whole of humanity, is both the judge of every aspect of its history and the savior rescuing it for a destiny of justice, peace, and reconciliation. Barmen, as we noted, made only the more modest claim that Christ's rule touched every area of the lives of Christians. Yet, confronted by God's judgment on Nazi Germany, the theologians of the GDR recognized that God claimed not only the lives of Christians, but the lives of all human beings.

We noted that this theme was developed at length by Heino Falcke, who presents Christ as the liberator of humanity. The principal aspect of this liberation is the freeing of believers from self-love and other fetters of the heart, enabling them to love, turn to their neighbor, transcend the inherited boundaries, extend solidarity to the poor, and assume responsibility for society as a whole. While Christ also frees the church for its mission and summons it to support the liberation of the oppressed, the principal liberation takes place in the lives of individuals. Falcke offers a theology of Christ's kingship that fully acknowledges justification by faith and the gratuity of salvation. The freedom to forget oneself and love the neighbor is not merited, but is freely communicated with the gift of faith. At the same time, the freedom to love the other does not enable believers to escape the ambiguity of life, for the decisions prompted by this love may turn out to serve someone else's evil purpose. Christians therefore remain justified sinners. But instead of permitting this Protestant doctrine to weaken confidence in social engagement and public involvement, Falcke interprets it in the context of Christ's liberating mission and hence as a summons to commitment and solidarity.

A second theme present in the Kirchenbund's theology was derived from Dietrich Bonhoeffer's understanding of faith as discipleship. Here the emphasis is not so much on the glorified Christ, as on the historical Christ — the Christ of the Beatitudes, the Man for others. For Bonhoeffer, faith was a praxis, a following of Jesus, a new life — granted freely and undeservedly — making believers "be" for others. For Bonhoeffer, the church itself was only church if it was church-for-others. This theology strongly affected Albrecht Schönherr, flowed into the Weissensee study circle, and influenced the self-definition of the Kirchenbund as a community of witness and service. A church that existed for others stopped dreaming of its high status in the past and did not resent the loss of its privileges: such a church recognized the need for conversion and willingly entered upon a new beginning in the socialist society. Such a church supported political efforts that aimed at enhancing people's material well-being and readily criticized policies that had damaging effects upon them. To be church-for-others in the GDR meant walking on the ridge between total refusal and total conformity.

At the same time, Schönherr did not forget the gratuity of salvation. According to Bonhoeffer, discipleship in the modern era, in the world become of age, implied the entry into social responsibility for the whole. For Bonhoeffer — and Schönherr after him — the gift of faith made people assume the burden of analyzing their own and the world's situation, taking into consideration the various historical currents, evaluating them as to their human consequences, participating in the suffering of the unjustly treated, and finally deciding upon their course of action. Christians thus acting responsibly are justified by faith — even if their decision turns out not to have been a good one. In this faith, Bonhoeffer decided to join the conspiracy against Hitler. Practicing discipleship in responsible decisions leaves Christians as forgiven sinners in the ambiguity of life. In this faith, the churchmen in the GDR decided to follow the path of critical solidarity — in humility, realizing that their judgment was not infallible, but trusting that they were justified by faith.

A third important theme influential in the theology of the Bund was the interpretation of God's promised shalom, taken from the ecumenical proposals developed at the WCC. Here the messianic promises of peace in the Old Testament, confirmed and fulfilled by Christ in the New, are understood as the revelation of humanity's divinely appointed destiny to live in peace, justice, and mutual respect and to practice compassion and stewardship of the earth. Because God loves the world, God's mission is to establish this shalom on earth. The church summoned to serve this divine mission must abandon an ecclesiocentric understanding of its ministry and stop thinking of itself as the object of God's first love. God loves the world, and because God is at work in human history in a hidden way, the church must be shalom-centred, ready to support the efforts of people wherever they may be to realize the promised shalom in their social existence. Here too the church is seen as church-for-others. Yet God's shalom is not only the vision that helps the church discern what social efforts deserve support, it is also the measure that allows the church to judge the existing societies and articulate their transgressions. In the GDR, the critical power of the theology of shalom was brought out by the Dresden Report of the Conciliar Process.

We also noted that the theology of shalom and the *missio Dei* proposed in various ecumenical documents were received by Werner Krusche with a certain reservation, pointing out that humanity is in a situation of sin and that the power to establish shalom becomes available only through a gratuitous gift of forgiveness and new life. The Protestant theology in the GDR hinted at the presence of God's saving action among non-Christians, but it never clearly committed itself to this position. These theologians certainly held that because God ruled the world, good things did happen in human history; but they were more comfortable with a discourse that distinguished this earthly realm from the spiritual one. Even Bonhoeffer distinguished between justice in the world, "the penultimate," and reconciliation with God, "the ultimate." It is my impression that the Protestant theology in the GDR was unclear in regard to this important issue. On the one hand, it wanted to remain faithful to the Protestant doctrine of salvation through conscious, believing contact with Christ alone; and on the other, it admired the selflessness of non-Christians and marvelled at the sacrifices made by them, and hence tried to avoid any statement that made the church appear superior or better or more beloved than the world, allowing Christians to address society as it were from above.

These three theological themes, "Christ's universal relevance," "faith as discipleship," and "God's promised shalom" are not in contradiction with one another. They confirm one another, and in the theology of the Kirchenbund are skillfully woven together. We noted that the Bund avoided direct references to the two traditional doctrines of Christ's kingship and the two kingdoms, that its appeal to Christ's relevance to every area of human existence was drawn from Barmen, and that in its own way, it remained faithful to the gratuity and inwardness of the life of faith that the doctrine of the two kingdoms intended to protect.

* * *

We also noted in this study that the major theologians — Falcke, Krusche, Schönherr — as well as the Kirchenbund avoided the one-sidedness associated with a radical interpretation of the above-mentioned theological themes. I mentioned Krusche's correction of the *missio Dei* theology. Despite the Protestant *solus,* these theologians always sought a balance and added a little "and" of their own. Schönherr rejected a one-sided interpretation of Bonhoeffer, justified by certain of his texts, according to which Christianity was about to become entirely religionless. Schönherr explained that Bonhoeffer was a man of prayer and that for him discipleship meant prayer and the dedication to justice. The response to the divine call does not exhaust itself in the service of the world, but includes a new relationship to God sustained by prayer. Public worship should strengthen the church for its mission, but worship is more than that; it relates the church to God in repentance and thanksgiving. That is why Krusche, commenting on Hoekendijk's theology, wrote that church is indeed mission, but it is not only mission. Schönherr warned against interpreting Bonhoeffer's message as a theological horizontalism.

Bonhoeffer — and Schönherr after him — vehemently rejected metaphysics in the name of "the one reality," earthly and historical, to which we belong and in which God is present. Yet Bonhoeffer, facing execution by hanging, firmly believed that he would live with God. Schönherr also relativized "the one reality" by his faith in the resurrection. The theologians of the Kirchenbund were open to and influenced by several radical theological trends, but by qualifying them, they remained in the orthodox tradition of their church.

Nor did the theologians follow a one-sided interpretation of the church-for-others. We noted that in the seventies, the Bund became aware that emphasizing the church's witness and service made excessive demands on the local congregations and neglected the church's pastoral ministry to its own members. To correct this situation, the Bund developed pastoral programs for parishioners of all walks of life, helping them to define their identity and to find the right path in the socialist society. The theologians recognized that the church can "be" for others and extend its solidarity to all who seek justice only if it has an intense spiritual existence supported by silence, inwardness, and care. We saw that the ecumenical discourse of *Sendung* and *Sammlung* (mission and gathering/recollection) tried to deal with this issue. What the theologians implied, but did not clearly articulate, is that for the church to be for others, it also has to be — in the right way — for itself.

That serving the church's own need is not to be a betrayal of the church-for-others was recognized by the Kirchenbund in its struggle to obtain a free space for its own activities in the socialist state. Since the discourse of the church-for-others does not fully justify this self-concern, it is perhaps not surprising that members of the Pfarrerbund, close to the government as they were, looked upon the noble language of the "church as servant" as a disguise for the Protestant Church's renewed quest for power. They were wrong in this supposition, but they were right in sensing that a discourse of total selflessness does not do justice to what is needed to love and serve others. If the *agape* of the New Testament excluded all self-love, then self-concern, even if it is the church's, would be self-indulgent; then striving for a free social space in the GDR would be sinful. But the Kirchenbund did not think so. Without touching on the classical theological debate regarding the relation of *agape* and self-concern, the Bund kept an even keel. I conclude — with admiration — that despite the radicalness of its discourse and the boldness of its chosen path, Protestant theology in the GDR never lost its balance.

*　　*　　*

The issue of the relationship between self-love and other-love brings to light an important difference between the Protestant theology in East Germany and Latin American liberation theology. Both of these theologies were contextual, both were action-oriented, both believed that faith had political implications, both expressed solidarity with the poor, and both affirmed "the one reality" while believing in the glory of the life to come. Yet there were significant differences between these two theologies.

The Protestant theologians in the GDR understood faith as discipleship, as being for others, as seeking justice and extending solidarity to the poor. Even though they lived in the GDR, a country of modest means, they saw themselves as belonging to the rich sector of the world, summoned by God to abandon their self-concern and turn to their neighbor, especially the poor and underprivileged. In this context, self-love or self-interest appeared to them as sinful.

By contrast, for the poor of Latin America, faith meant believing that though the world rejected them, God in Christ has graciously accepted them. God stood with them, God enabled them to affirm themselves, to overcome passivity, self-doubt, and the false scruples induced by church preaching, and to demand their place under the sun in the face of the wicked world that excluded them. The option for the poor was here an option for themselves. Conversion here meant abandoning the self-contempt mediated to them by church and culture and receiving the new self-esteem mediated by the gospel. Thanks to Jesus, the poor were now able to love themselves and reach out for the material and spiritual goods they needed to escape from the structures that imprisoned them. The love of God taught them to love themselves rightly. Fearful and timid before, they now were divinely graced to stand up for themselves. Sin, for them, was not self-interest and self-reliance; but on the contrary, sin was above all the return to the self-contempt and powerlessness they had experienced in the past. Of course they interpreted the call to pursue their own interest not in an individualistic way, but collectively referring to the entire community. Their liberation struggle — even if it only meant getting access to clean water — was motivated by the love of God's justice as well as by their material self-interest. These few remarks reveal that the church-for-others theology of the developed world has a different internal structure from the liberation theologies of oppressed peoples.

Another difference between the Protestant theology in the GDR and Latin American liberation theology was that the word *socialism* had a different meaning for them. In the GDR, socialism was the name of the existing society and its official ideology imposed by law. We saw that apart from a small group, Christians in the GDR never called themselves socialist. Although the Bund recognized the affinity between socialism's humanistic ideals and the divine promises in the Scriptures, it emphasized the unbridgeable gap between the Christian and the socialist vision of the world. They called themselves the church *in* socialism, never *for* socialism.

In the Latin American liberation theology, at least until a few years ago, socialism referred to the alternative society that the poor and those in solidarity with them wanted to build. Latin Americans spoke of their historical project as a collective effort to escape the world capitalist system and construct societies that would give work to their people and enable them to feed and house their families. Latin Americans were not attracted by Soviet bloc socialism. They dreamed of a populist, nonbureaucratic, decentralized socialism, open to the participation of local communities. In Latin American liberation theology, socialism referred, not to a perfect society in which all injustices were overcome, but simply to a more just society, qualitatively different from the present. This socialist society did not as yet exist, but they believed that its construction was close enough to the historical possibilities of the present that struggling for it was not an unrealistic endeavor.

In Latin America and Western Europe, Christians who looked upon the capitalist economy as a sinful structure often called themselves Marxists. For them Marxism did not refer to a single intellectual or political orientation, but to a spectrum of options, all of which regarded the master/slave relation in the economic order as the starting point of their critical reflections. These Christians called themselves Marxists as others had called themselves Platonists or Aristotelians, without thereby locking themselves into a fixed system of thought. By contrast, in Communist East Germany, as we saw above, Marxism or more precisely Marxism-Leninism was the officially defined and imposed ideology, and the Christians of the Bund acknowledged the unbridgeable gap between that ideology and Christian faith.

Let me add that Latin American liberation theology, being for the most part of Catholic origin, accepted more readily than did the Protestant theology that revealed in Jesus Christ was God's gracious presence in the whole of humanity, enabling people to leave their destructive past behind and move into a new, more life-giving future. God stands with the poor wherever they are. In liberation theology, human history was seen as supernatural since God was creatively and redemptively involved in it. At the same time, liberation theology — as much as the Protestant theology in the GDR — eschewed evolutionary ideas of any kind, as if God had promised the final reconciliation of humanity within history. The entry of a people into greater justice in one generation may be undone by human sin in the next. Even societies that do much to serve the common good depend daily upon God's mercy.

*   *   *

Christians in East Germany, as we saw above, believed that their socialist society was reformable. From the seventies on, they experienced a more open attitude of the government toward the church. We mentioned the agreement of March 6, 1978, which gave the Protestant Church a certain freedom and a new presence in the socialist society. Some Christians were critical of Bishop Schönherr's and the Bund's diplomatic efforts: they argued that the institutional advantages for the

Church gained by negotiations left unchanged the discrimination experienced by Christians at the base. Schönherr himself recognized this danger. He constantly pointed out to the government, even in the address at the meeting of March 6, 1978, that "the relation between church and state is as good as it is experienced by Christian citizens in their own local situation."[1] Still, the fact that the state had significantly modified its attitude toward the church was recognized by both Protestants and Catholics. In 1981 the Protestant leadership conference acknowledged this in a formal way.[2]

Christian observers in the GDR noticed, moreover, that Marxist thinkers began to look differently upon religion.[3] Marxists argued that in a developed socialism there was no need for the state to oppose religion in an active manner. Religion remains at odds with the Marxist perception of reality; but this difference is no longer an antithetical contradiction to be overcome by ruthless struggle, but a nonantithetical contradiction that allows for peaceful cooperation in the building of the socialist society. Some Marxist thinkers in the GDR explained that since religion now supported economic equality and international peace — referring to the WCC and the East German Church — they no longer found convincing the classical Marxist view of religion as false consciousness and consolation for the oppressed. They now saw religion as rooted in the profound human desire to cope with suffering and death, search for a unified meaning in their personal existence, and experience acceptance and a feeling of being at home in the universe. Since the socialist society will evolve only gradually to the point where it is able to deliver people from all alienation, religion will accompany socialism for a long time.

Christian observers in the GDR also noticed that the official commemoration of Luther's birthday in 1983 was accompanied by an

1. Albrecht Schönherr, *Abenteuer der Nachfolge. Reden und Aufsätze, 1978-1988* (Berlin: Wichern-Verlag, 1988), 276.

2. *Gemeinsam unterwegs. Dokumente aus der Arbeit des BEK in der DDR* (Berlin: Evangelische Verlagsanstalt, 1989), 309.

3. Schönherr, 306-307; Konrad Feiereis, "Zusammenleben und Kooperation von Christen und Marxisten in der Gesellschaft" (a paper given at "Christen und Marxisten im Dialog," Budapest, 1986), in *Unter kommunistischer Zensur,* Theologisches Jahrbuch 1991, ed. W. Ernst et al. (Leipzig: Benno Verlag, 1986), 357-371.

extensive Marxist literature that not only saw in Luther the reactionary defender of the feudal order, but also appreciated the emphasis of his preaching on service to the neighbor, creative and meaningful work, the protection of the family, and the virtues of diligence, frugality, and the fulfillment of duty.[4] These authors regretted that ethics had been neglected in Marxist thought, certainly since Karl Kautsky, and suggested that it was high time to repair this lacuna. Marxists authors began to show an interest in ethical issues such as friendship and personal integrity.

The government itself was divided between hard-liners and the more conciliatory. The state ministry for church questions, especially under Klaus Gysi, was tolerant of religion, opposed social discrimination against Christian believers, and recognized that granting the churches a free space would make their members better citizens. Horst Dohle, who worked in this ministry, claims that since the ruling party, the SED, had their own secretary for church questions, usually a hard-liner, the ministry had little influence on the government.[5] Reformists in the GDR were also encouraged by the joint document of August 27, 1987, produced by the SED and the West German social-democratic party (SPD), dealing with the conflict between ideologies and the common concern for peace and security.[6]

Knowledge of the new trends in Marxist thinking and the realization that the government itself was divided on many issues encouraged Christians — and other citizens — to believe in the possibility of reforming the existing socialism. We saw that the dissident groups organized in the local congregations were not attracted by Western capitalist culture, but believed in the possibility of a socialism with a human face. When in the eighties, masses of East Germans tried to leave the country for the West, Protestant church leaders and even Catholic bishops tried to discourage the members of their churches

4. Götz Planer-Friedrich, "Luthererinnerungen und Gemeindeerneuerung," *Zeitschrift für evangelische Ethik* 29, 4 (1985): 371-408.

5. Horst Dohle, "Kirchen in der DDR: Möglichkeiten und verpasste Gelegenheiten echter Kooperation im Interesse des Humanum," *Berliner Dialog Hefte* 3 (1991): 34-49; 5 (1991): 17-33.

6. *Gemeinsam*, 220.

from running away.[7] They argued, with varying emphases, that Christians could be faithful to the gospel in the GDR, that they should not allow themselves to be tempted by West Germany's material wealth, and that their work and dedication were needed at home by their families and their country.

We recall here that in the GDR, right up to the turning point in October 1989, to be reformist in orientation was looked upon by the government as radical, heretical, and deserving unqualified condemnation. In this situation, the critical solidarity offered by the Kirchenbund was not a stabilizing factor in society: the bold path between total rejection and total acceptance produced reformist hopes that undermined the government's own self-understanding. Contemporary critics who claim that the Protestant policy of critical solidarity exercised a stabilizing influence in the GDR interpret this policy abstractly, lifted out of its historical context, where it questioned and thus destabilized the monopoly of the state.

From a different perspective, however, the practice of the Christian faith is undoubtedly a stabilizing factor in society. If Christian life includes being honest and caring, doing one's work with diligence, being reliable and helpful at one's job, having a stable family life, and not being driven by personal gain, then Christian life is surely a stabilizing force in any society. Even the Catholic bishops in the GDR recognized that their people made an important contribution to their society by leading good and dedicated lives. "Christians whose faith shapes the whole of their lives become a positive ferment in society, even our own," the Catholic bishops wrote in a pastoral letter of 1983. When Pope John Paul II visited East Germany in 1986, he liked the bishops' sentence so much that he repeated it in his own address.[8] Joachim Wanke, presently Catholic bishop of Erfurt, used to tease the men of the government by saying that their economy would work much better if they had more, rather than fewer dedicated Christians, and

7. Werner Krusche, "6 März: 1978-1988 ein Lernweg" (Berlin: Sekretariat, Bund der Evangelischen Kirchen, 1988), 14-16; Gerhard Lange et al., eds., *Katholische Kirche — Sozialistischer Staat DDR. Dokumente und öffentliche Aeusserungen, 1945-1990* (Leipzig: Benno Verlag, 1992), 301-305, 341-342, 362-374.
    8. Lange, 328, 366.

that their society would be properly socialist only if their citizens were all saints.[9]

The bishops and theologians of the Kirchenbund made a mistake, one in which they were accompanied by the vast majority of people in the world — politicians, social scientists, historians, journalists, and public opinion in general. They thought that the Communist societies of Eastern Europe were here to stay. Yet to everyone's surprise, these regimes collapsed. What happened to the Protestant Church and the citizens' movements after the collapse of the SED is beyond the scope of this book. When Jürgen Moltmann, the internationally known theologian from West Germany, visited East Germany after the reunification in 1991, he beseeched the East German Church: "Hold on to your identity, tell your dramatic story, remember and remind us of what has happened, put everything down in writing."[10]

9. Joachim Wanke, "Glaubenserfahrung aus der Zeit des DDR-Sozialismus," *Lebendiges Zeugnis* [Schriftreihe der Akademischen Bonifatius-Einigung, Paderborn] 47 (May 1992): 91.

10. Roland Degen, *Gemeindeerneuerung als gemeinpädagogische Aufgabe* (Münster/Berlin: Comenius-Institut, 1992), 7.

Bibliography

Adler, Elisabeth. "Freiheit in Grenzen: 40 Jahre Akademiearbeit in Berlin-Brandenburg," *Nachlese* [Berlin-Brandenburg: Evangelische Akademie] 1 (1992): 1-32.

Bassarak, Gerhard. "Heil heute und Wohl des Menschen." *Standpunkt* (October 1974): 201-207.

Baum, Gregory, and Robert Ellsberg, eds. *The Logic of Solidarity.* Maryknoll, NY: Orbis Books, 1979.

Bock, Hartmund. "Königsherrschaft Christi und Zweireichenlehre." *Standpunkt* (May 1973): 119-120.

Degen, Roland. *Gemeindeerneuerung als gemeinpädagogische Aufgabe.* Münster/Berlin: Comenius-Institut, 1992.

"Dieser Weg ist auch der unsere." *Standpunkt* (October 1974): 197.

Dohle, Horst. "Kirchen in der DDR: Möglichkeiten und verpasste Gelegenheiten echter Kooperation im Interesse des Humanum." *Berliner Dialog Hefte* 3 (1991): 34-49; 5 (1991): 17-33.

Falcke, Heino. *Mit Gott Schritt halten. Reden und Aufsätze.* Berlin: Wichern-Verlag, 1986.

Feiereis, Konrad. "Zusammenleben und Kooperation von Christen und Marxisten in der Gesellschaft." A paper given at "Christen und Marxisten im Dialog," Budapest, 1986. In *Unter kommunistischer Zensur,* Theologisches Jahrbuch 1991, ed. W. Ernst et al., 357-371. Leipzig: Benno Verlag, 1986.

Fierro, Alfredo. *The Militant Gospel.* Maryknoll, NY: Orbis Books, 1977.

Gemeinsam unterwegs. Dokumente aus der Arbeit des BEK in der DDR. Berlin: Evangelische Verlagsanstalt, 1989.

151

Goeckel, Robert F. *The Lutheran Church and the East-German State.* Ithaca, NY: Cornell University Press, 1990.

Henkys, Reinhard. *Bund der evangelischen Kirchen in der DDR. Dokumente zu seiner Entstehung.* Berlin: Eckart Verlag, 1970.

————. *Gottes Volk im Sozialismus.* Berlin: Wichern-Verlag, 1983.

————, ed. *Die Evangelische Kirche in der DDR.* München: Kaiser Verlag, 1982.

Hoekendijk, J. C. *The Church Inside Out.* Philadelphia: Westminster, 1966.

Jacob, Günter. *Der Christ in der sozialistischen Gesellschaft.* Stuttgart: Evangelische Verlagsanstalt, 1975.

————. *Kirche auf Wegen der Erneuerung.* Göttingen: Verlag Vandenhoeck, 1966.

————. *Weltwirklichkeit und Christusglaube.* Stuttgart: Evangelische Verlagsanstalt, 1977.

Jauch, Ernst-Alfred. "Katholische Kirche in der DDR." In *Kirche in der DDR,* Heft 1, ed. U.-P. Heidingsfeld, 39-54. Materialsstelle der Evangelisch-Lutherischen Kirche in Bayern, 1980.

Knauft, Wolfgang. *Katholische Kirche in der DDR, 1945-1980.* Mainz: Grünewald Verlag, 1980.

Kokschal, P. "Veröffentlichungen unter staatlicher Zensur." In *Unter kommunistischer Zensur,* Theologisches Jahrbuch 1991, ed. W. Ernst et al., 16-22. Leipzig: Benno Verlag, 1992.

Krusche, Werner. "Kirche in ideologischer Diaspora." *Kirche im Sozialismus* 1 (1974): 11-15.

————. "Kritische Solidarität: der Weg der evangelischen Kirchen in der DDR." *Theologische Studienabteilung.* Berlin: Bund der Evangelischen Kirchen, 1990.

————. "Rückblick auf 21 Jahre Weg- und Arbeitsgemeinschaft im Bund der Evangelischen Kirchen." Berlin: Sekretariat, Bund der Evangelischen Kirchen, 1991.

————. *Schritte und Markierungen. Aufsätze und Vorträge zum Weg der Kirche.* Berlin: Evangelische Verlagsanstallt, 1972.

————. "6 März: 1978-1988 ein Lernweg." Berlin: Sekretariat, Bund der Evangelischen Kirchen, 1988.

Lange, Gerhard, et al., eds. *Katholische Kirche — Sozialistischer Staat DDR. Dokumente und öffentliche Aeusserungen, 1945-1990.* Leipzig: Benno Verlag, 1992.

Lehtiö, Pirkko. *Religionsunterricht ohne Schule. Die Entwicklung der Lage und des Inhaltes der evangelischen Christenlehre in der DDR von 1945-1959.* Münster: Comenius-Institut, 1983.

Leipzig im Oktober. Kirchen und alternative Gruppen im Umbruch der DDR. Berlin: Wichern-Verlag, 1990.

Maleck, Bernhard. *Heinrich Fink*. Berlin: Dietz, 1992.

Oekumenische Versammlung für Gerechtigkeit, Frieden und Bewahrung der Schöpfung. Dresden-Magdeburg-Dresden, eine Dokumentation. Berlin: Aktion Sühnezeichen/Friedensdienste, 1990.

Osborn, Robert T. *The Barmen Declaration as a Paradigm for a Theology of the American Church*. Lewiston, NY: Edwin Mellen Press, 1991.

Planer-Friedrich, Götz. "Luthererinnerungen und Gemeindeerneuerung." *Zeitschrift für evangelische Ethik* 29, 4 (1985): 371-408.

Ratzmann, W. *Missionarische Gemeinde*. Berlin: Evangelische Verlagsanstalt, 1980.

Rein, Gerhard, ed. *Die Opposition in der DDR. Entwürfe für einen anderen Sozialismus*. Berlin: Wichern-Verlag, 1989.

————. *Die Protestantische Revolution, 1987-1989*. Berlin: Wichern-Verlag, 1990.

Röder, Hans-Jürgen. "Kirche im Sozialismus." In *Die Evangelische Kirche in der DDR*, ed. Reinhard Henkys, 62-85. München: Kaiser Verlag, 1982.

Schabowski, Günter. *Der Absturz*. Berlin: Rowohl, 1991.

Scharf, Kurt. *Brücken und Breschen. Biographische Skizzen*. Berlin: C. Z. V. Verlag, 1977.

Scheidacker, Werner. "30 Jahre Kirche in der DDR." *Die Zeichen der Zeit* 10 (1979): 361-368.

Schönherr, Albrecht. *Abenteuer der Nachfolge. Reden und Aufsätze, 1978-1988*. Berlin: Wichern-Verlag, 1988.

————. *Horizont und Mitte. Aufsätze, Vorträge, Reden, 1953-1977*. München: Chr. Kaiser Verlag, 1979.

————. "Ueber Auftrag und Weg der Kirche Jesu Christi in der sozialisten Gesellschaft der DDR." *Die Zeichen der Zeit* 4 (1979): 369-379.

————. "Weder Opportunismus noch Opposition," *Die Zeit* (February 7, 1992), Politik, 4.

Schorlemmer, Friedrich. *Worte öffnen Fäuste*. München: Kindler-Verlag, 1992.

Schröder, Richard. "Was kann 'Kirche im Sozialismus' sinvoll heissen." *Kirche im Sozialismus* 4 (1988): 135-137.

Stawinski, Reinhard. "Theologie in der DDR — DDR Theologie?" In *Die Evangelische Kirche in der DDR*, ed. Reinhard Henkys, 86-110. München: Kaiser Verlag, 1982.

Stolpe, Manfred. *Den Menschen Hoffnung geben. Reden, Aufsätze, Interviews*. Berlin: Wichern-Verlag, 1991.

Stransky, Tom. "Missio Dei." In *Dictionary of the Ecumenical Movement*, 687-689. Geneva: WCC Publications, 1991.

Triebler, Wolfgang, ed. *Die Erlöserkirche, Berlin-Lichtenberg, 1892-1992*. A book published by this congregation, 1992.

Voigt, Gottfried. "Bekennen und dienen: 30 Jahre Kirche in der DDR." *Die Zeichen der Zeit* 4 (1979): 380-384.

Wanke, Joachim. "Glaubenserfahrung aus der Zeit des DDR-Sozialismus." *Lebendiges Zeugnis* [Schriftreihe der Akademischen Bonifatius-Einigung, Paderborn, 47] (May 1992): 85-94.

————. *Last und Chance des Christseins.* Leipzig: Benno Verlag, 1991.

Zander, Ruth. "Zum Gebrauch des Begriffes Kirche im Sozialismus." Berlin: Bund der Evangelischen Kirchen, 1988.

Index